Better Homes and Gardens®

MORE easy everyday COOKING

Better Homes and Gardens® Books
Des Moines, Iowa

Copyright © 2003 by Meredith Corporation, Des Moines, Iowa. First Edition. All rights reserved. Printed in the United States of America. Library of Congress Control Number: 2002109234 ISBN: 0-696-21626-4

Pictured on front cover: Zesty Vegetable Enchiladas (see recipe, page 197)

Better Homes and Gardens® Books
An imprint of Meredith® Books

More Easy Everyday Cooking
Editor: Carrie E. Holcomb
Contributing Editor: Spectrum Communication Services, Inc.
Contributing Designer: Seif Visual Communications
Copy Chief: Terri Fredrickson
Copy and Production Editor: Victoria Forlini
Editorial Operations Manager: Karen Schirm
Managers, Book Production: Pam Kvitne, Marjorie J. Schenkelberg
Contributing Copy Editor: Kim Catanzarite
Contributing Proofreaders: Gretchen Kauffman, Susan J. Kling, Donna Segal
Electronic Production Coordinator: Paula Forest
Editorial and Design Assistants: Mary Lee Gavin, Karen McFadden
Test Kitchen Director: Lynn Blanchard
Test Kitchen Product Supervisor: Marilyn Cornelius

Meredith® Books
Editor in Chief: Linda Raglan Cunningham
Design Director: Matt Strelecki
Executive Editor, Food and Crafts: Jennifer Dorland Darling

Publisher: James D. Blume
Executive Director, Marketing: Jeffrey Myers
Executive Director, New Business Development: Todd M. Davis
Executive Director, Sales: Ken Zagor
Director, Operations: George A. Susral
Director, Production: Douglas M. Johnston
Business Director: Jim Leonard

Vice President and General Manager: Douglas J. Guendel

Better Homes and Gardens® Magazine
Editor in Chief: Karol DeWulf Nickell
Deputy Editor, Food and Entertaining: Nancy Hopkins

Meredith Publishing Group
President, Publishing Group: Stephen M. Lacy
Vice President–Publishing Director: Bob Mate

Meredith Corporation
Chairman and Chief Executive Officer: William T. Kerr

Chairman of the Executive Committee: E. T. Meredith III

SIMPLE AND QUICK FAMILY-PLEASING RECIPES!

Anyone who cooks knows that preparing satisfying meals for your family day in and day out is a challenge. The same meals you once loved become the old, boring reliables over time, yet it's hard to break out of the rut. With *More Easy Everyday Cooking*, putting dinner on the table is easier. Brimming with more than 200 versatile recipes, this captivating volume includes great-tasting ways to prepare everything from appetizers to desserts. Even Horseradish-Dill Beef Stroganoff, Swiss Chicken Bundles, or Sweet Pepper Salsa Fish can be easy and everyday! To end the meal, you'll find dozens of enticing treats: Fruit Chip Cookies, Deep Chocolate Cake with Malt Topping, and Peach and Almond Crisp, just to name a few.

Don't hesitate—try a tantalizing new recipe from *More Easy Everyday Cooking* tonight. You'll be glad you did.

Contents

Appetizers
& SNACKS

Contents

LAYERED SOUTHWESTERN DIP
(recipe, page 8)

Cowboy Caviar

Scoop up some of this salsalike appetizer with a tortilla chip or cracker.

1   15-ounce can black-eyed peas, rinsed and drained
¼   cup thinly sliced green onions
¼   cup finely chopped red sweet pepper
2   tablespoons cooking oil
2   tablespoons cider vinegar
1   or 2 fresh jalapeño peppers, seeded and chopped
2   cloves garlic, minced
¼   teaspoon cracked black pepper
    Dash salt
    Tortilla chips or assorted crackers

In a medium bowl combine black-eyed peas, green onions, sweet pepper, oil, vinegar, jalapeño peppers, garlic, black pepper, and salt. Cover and chill overnight.

To serve, transfer to a serving dish. Serve with tortilla chips or crackers. Makes about 2 cups.

Nutrition information per tablespoon dip: 18 cal., 1 g total fat (0 g sat. fat), 0 mg chol., 21 mg sodium, 2 g carbo., 1 g pro.

Berry Good Fruit Dip

Pureed strawberries flavor a mixture of vanilla yogurt and whipped topping. Serve with fruit fanned around the bowl of dip.

1   cup strawberries
¾   cup fat-free vanilla yogurt
½   teaspoon ground cinnamon
¼   teaspoon ground ginger
½   of an 8-ounce container frozen light whipped dessert topping, thawed
    Apple wedges, pear wedges, whole strawberries, or other fruit dippers

Place the strawberries in a blender container or food processor bowl. Cover and blend or process until smooth.

In a medium bowl stir together the pureed strawberries, yogurt, cinnamon, and ginger. Fold in the dessert topping. Cover and chill up to 24 hours.

To serve, transfer to a serving dish. Serve with fresh fruit dippers. Makes 12 servings.

Nutrition information per serving (dip only): 38 cal., 1 g total fat (0 g sat. fat), 1 mg chol., 17 mg sodium, 6 g carbo., 1 g pro.

Cowboy Caviar

Layered Southwestern Dip

If you want a real crowd pleaser, these seven layers of fresh, colorful Mexican flavors do the trick.

2 cups shredded lettuce
1 15-ounce can reduced-sodium
   black beans, rinsed and drained
½ cup chopped green sweet pepper
2 tablespoons bottled chopped red
   jalapeño peppers or canned
   diced green chile peppers
1 8-ounce carton fat-free dairy
   sour cream
1 8-ounce jar chunky salsa
½ cup shredded reduced-fat cheddar
   cheese (2 ounces)
2 tablespoons chopped pitted
   ripe olives
   Homemade Tortilla Chips

Line a 12-inch platter with shredded lettuce. In a medium bowl stir together black beans, green sweet pepper, and jalapeño peppers or green chile peppers. Spoon over lettuce, leaving a border of lettuce. Spoon sour cream over bean mixture; gently spread in a smooth layer, leaving a border of bean mixture.

Drain excess liquid from salsa. Spoon salsa over sour cream layer, leaving a border of sour cream. Sprinkle cheese over salsa; top with olives. If desired, cover and chill up to 6 hours. Serve with Homemade Tortilla Chips. Makes 24 servings.

Homemade Tortilla Chips: Cut each of sixteen 7- to 8-inch flour tortillas into 6 wedges. Arrange wedges in a single layer on ungreased baking sheets. Bake in a 350° oven for 10 to 15 minutes or until dry and crisp. Makes 96 chips.

Nutrition information per serving: 80 cal., 2 g total fat (1 g sat. fat), 2 mg chol., 178 mg sodium, 12 g carbo., 3 g pro.

Bruschetta

Italians created these toasted and topped appetizers for the distinct purpose of using up day-old bread.

1	cup pitted ripe olives
2	teaspoons balsamic vinegar or red wine vinegar
2	cloves garlic, minced
1	teaspoon capers, drained
1	teaspoon olive oil
1⅓	cups chopped red and/or yellow tomatoes (2 medium)
⅓	cup thinly sliced green onions
1	tablespoon snipped fresh basil or oregano or 1 teaspoon dried basil or oregano, crushed
1	tablespoon olive oil
⅛	teaspoon pepper
1	8-ounce loaf baguette-style French bread
2	tablespoons olive oil
½	cup grated or finely shredded Parmesan cheese

For olive paste, in a food processor bowl or blender container combine olives, vinegar, garlic, capers, and the 1 teaspoon olive oil. Cover and process or blend until a nearly smooth paste forms, stopping and scraping the sides as necessary.

For topping, in a small bowl stir together chopped tomatoes, green onions, basil or oregano, the 1 tablespoon olive oil, and the pepper.

For toast, cut bread into ½-inch slices. Using the 2 tablespoons olive oil, lightly brush both sides of each bread slice with oil. Place on an ungreased baking sheet. Bake in a 425° oven about 5 minutes or until crisp and light brown, turning once.

To assemble, spread each piece of toast with a thin layer of olive paste. Top each with about 2 tablespoons of the topping; sprinkle with Parmesan cheese. Return slices to the ungreased baking sheet. Bake for 2 to 3 minutes more or until cheese starts to melt and topping is heated through. Serve warm. Makes 24 appetizers.

Nutrition information per appetizer: 62 cal., 4 g total fat (1 g sat. fat), 2 mg chol., 125 mg sodium, 6 g carbo., 2 g pro.

Brie en Croûte

Jalapeño pepper jelly adds zing to this rich, buttery appetizer.

½ of a 17.3-ounce package (1 sheet)
   frozen puff pastry sheets, thawed
2 tablespoons jalapeño pepper jelly
2 4½-ounce rounds Brie or
   Camembert cheese
2 tablespoons chopped nuts, toasted
1 slightly beaten egg
1 tablespoon water
   Apple and/or pear slices

Grease a baking sheet; set aside. Unfold pastry on a lightly floured surface; roll pastry into a 16×10-inch rectangle. Using an 8-inch round cake pan as a pattern, cut pastry into two 8-inch circles; reserve pastry trimmings.

Spread jelly over top of cheese rounds. Sprinkle with nuts; lightly press nuts into jelly. In a small bowl combine egg and water; set aside.

Place pastry circles on top of cheese rounds. Invert cheese and pastry together. Brush edges of pastry with egg mixture; pleat and pinch edges to cover and seal. Trim excess pastry. Place rounds, smooth sides up, on the prepared baking sheet. Brush egg mixture over tops and sides. Cut small slits for steam to escape. Using hors d'oeuvre cutters, cut shapes from reserved pastry. Brush shapes with egg mixture; place on top of rounds.

Bake in a 400° oven for 20 to 25 minutes or until pastry is deep golden brown. Let stand for 10 to 20 minutes before serving. Serve with apple and/or pear slices. Makes 12 servings.

Nutrition information per serving: 193 cal., 14 g total fat (4 g sat. fat), 38 mg chol., 216 mg sodium, 13 g carbo., 6 g pro.

TOASTING NUTS

Toasting heightens the flavor of nuts. To toast, spread the nuts in a single layer in a shallow baking pan. Bake in a 350° oven for 5 to 10 minutes or until light golden brown, watching carefully and stirring once or twice so nuts don't burn.

Popcorn 'n' Cranberry Snack Mix

The goodies tend to sink to the bottom, so stir occasionally while serving.

1   package unpopped microwave
        popcorn
     Nonstick cooking spray
2   to 3 tablespoons grated Parmesan
        cheese
2   cups potato sticks
1½   cups soy nuts
1   cup dried cranberries or mixed
        dried fruit

Pop popcorn according to package directions. Pour popcorn into a very large bowl; coat lightly with cooking spray.

Sprinkle popcorn with Parmesan cheese; toss gently to coat. Stir in potato sticks, soy nuts, and dried cranberries or mixed dried fruit. Makes 12 servings.

Nutrition information per serving: 169 cal., 7 g total fat (2 g sat. fat), 1 mg chol., 159 mg sodium, 21 g carbo., 7 g pro.

Cinnamon Bagel Chips

These crisp and crunchy snacks make great treats for kids as well as grown-ups.

3   unsplit plain, cinnamon-raisin, egg,
        sesame, or poppy seed bagels
2   teaspoons cooking oil
2   tablespoons sugar
1   teaspoon ground cinnamon
¼   teaspoon ground nutmeg

Slice bagels from top to bottom into ⅛-inch slices. Arrange bagel slices on an ungreased baking sheet. Brush very lightly with oil. Bake in a 325° oven for 20 to 25 minutes or until toasted.

In a plastic bag combine the sugar, cinnamon, and nutmeg. Add hot bagel slices; seal bag. Toss chips until coated with spice mixture. Shake off excess coating. Cool chips before serving. Makes about 36 chips.

Nutrition information per chip: 21 cal., 0 g total fat (0 g sat. fat), 0 mg chol., 32 mg sodium, 4 g carbo., 1 g pro.

Steamed Beef Dumplings

Steaming, a timeless Oriental cooking method, keeps the fat in these tasty bite-size morsels to a minimum.

2 cups all-purpose flour
½ teaspoon salt
⅔ cup boiling water
¼ cup cold water
2 tablespoons bottled hoisin sauce or reduced-sodium soy sauce
1 teaspoon cornstarch
1 cup finely chopped bok choy
1 medium carrot, shredded (½ cup)
2 tablespoons thinly sliced green onion
2 tablespoons snipped fresh cilantro
¼ teaspoon salt
12 ounces lean ground beef
  Soy Dipping Sauce
  Fresh cilantro (optional)

In a medium bowl stir together flour and the ½ teaspoon salt. Using a fork, stir in the boiling water. Add the cold water; mix with your hands until the dough forms a ball. (The dough will be sticky.) Cover and set aside.

For filling, in another medium bowl stir together hoisin or soy sauce and cornstarch. Stir in bok choy, carrot, green onion, the 2 tablespoons cilantro, and the ¼ teaspoon salt. Add ground beef; mix well. Using about 1 tablespoon filling for each, shape into 30 balls.

Divide dough in half. Return one portion to the bowl; cover and set aside. Divide the other portion into 15 balls. On a well-floured surface, roll each ball into a 3-inch circle. Place a ball of filling in the center of each dough circle. Fold each dough circle up and around filling, allowing the filling to show at the top. Press dough firmly around filling, pleating to fit. Gently flatten the bottom of each dumpling. Repeat with the remaining dough and filling.

In a steamer or Dutch oven bring water to boiling. Place dumplings, open sides up, on a greased steamer rack, making sure the edges don't touch. (If all the dumplings won't fit on a steamer rack, chill remainder until ready to steam.) Place rack over, but not touching, boiling water. Cover and steam dumplings for 16 to 18 minutes or until meat is done (160°). Serve warm with Soy Dipping Sauce. If desired, garnish with additional cilantro. Makes 30 appetizers.

Soy Dipping Sauce: In a small bowl combine ¼ cup rice vinegar or white vinegar and ¼ cup reduced-sodium soy sauce. Sprinkle with 1 teaspoon thinly sliced green onion.

Nutrition information per appetizer: 54 cal., 1 g total fat (1 g sat. fat), 7 mg chol., 201 mg sodium, 7 g carbo., 3 g pro.

Tuscan-Style Stuffed Chicken Breasts

If you wish, serve each pinwheel on a thin slice of crusty bread with mustard.

4	medium skinless, boneless chicken breast halves (about 1 pound total)
4	ounces fontina cheese, crumbled or sliced
1	cup bottled roasted red sweet peppers
12	fresh sage leaves or 1 teaspoon dried sage, crushed
¼	cup all-purpose flour
2	tablespoons olive oil
1	cup dry white wine or chicken broth

Place each chicken piece between two pieces of plastic wrap. Pound lightly with the flat side of a meat mallet until about ¼ inch thick. Remove plastic wrap. Sprinkle chicken with black pepper. For each roll, place one-fourth of the cheese, roasted peppers, and sage on a chicken piece. Fold in sides; roll up chicken. Roll in flour to coat.

In a large skillet cook chicken rolls in hot oil over medium heat about 5 minutes or until brown on all sides. Remove from skillet. Add wine or broth to skillet. Bring to boiling; reduce heat. Simmer, uncovered, about 2 minutes or until liquid is reduced to about ½ cup. Return chicken to skillet. Cover and simmer for 7 to 8 minutes or until chicken is no longer pink. To serve, trim ends of chicken rolls. Cut rolls into ¾-inch slices. Makes 16 appetizers.

Nutrition information per appetizer: 86 cal., 4 g total fat (2 g sat. fat), 25 mg chol., 72 mg sodium, 2 g carbo., 9 g pro.

Coffee Candied Nuts

These candy-coated nuts, with just a hint of coffee flavor, make a tasteful hostess gift.

1	egg white
1	tablespoon water
2	teaspoons instant espresso coffee powder or 4 teaspoons instant coffee crystals
½	cup sugar
3	cups salted mixed nuts (no peanuts)

Line a 15×10×1-inch baking pan with foil; grease foil. Set pan aside. In a large bowl beat together the egg white, water, and espresso powder or coffee crystals with a fork until powder is dissolved. Stir in sugar. Add nuts; stir to coat. Spread mixture in the prepared pan.

Bake in a 300° oven for 25 to 30 minutes or until coating becomes stiff and mixture is somewhat difficult to stir, stirring occasionally. Spread on a piece of lightly greased foil to cool. Break into pieces. Store, tightly covered, at room temperature. Makes 14 servings.

Nutrition information per serving: 218 cal., 17 g total fat (3 g sat. fat), 0 mg chol., 220 mg sodium, 14 g carbo., 5 g pro.

Tuscan-Style Stuffed Chicken Breasts

Mini Spinach Calzones

Refrigerated pizza dough takes the work out of these cheesy pizza pockets, while spinach and reduced-fat cream cheese make a filling that's good for you.

½ of a 10-ounce package frozen chopped spinach, thawed and well drained

½ of an 8-ounce package reduced-fat cream cheese (Neufchâtel), softened

2 tablespoons finely chopped green onion

1 tablespoon grated Parmesan cheese
Dash pepper

1 10-ounce package refrigerated pizza dough

1 tablespoon milk
Bottled light spaghetti sauce, warmed (optional)

Line a baking sheet with foil; lightly grease the foil. Set baking sheet aside. For filling, in a medium bowl stir together spinach, cream cheese, green onion, Parmesan cheese, and pepper. Set aside.

Unroll pizza dough on a lightly floured surface; roll dough into a 15-inch square. Using a knife, cut into twenty-five 3-inch squares. Spoon 1 rounded teaspoon filling onto each square. Brush edges of dough with water. Lift a corner of each square and stretch dough over filling to opposite corner, making a triangle. Press edges with fingers or a fork to seal.

Arrange the calzones on the prepared baking sheet. Prick tops of calzones with a fork. Brush with milk. Bake in a 425° oven for 8 to 10 minutes or until golden brown. Let stand for 5 minutes before serving. If desired, serve with spaghetti sauce. Makes 25 appetizers.

Nutrition information per appetizer: 38 cal., 2 g total fat (1 g sat. fat), 4 mg chol., 63 mg sodium, 5 g carbo., 1 g pro.

Mounds-of-Mushrooms Pizza

Mushrooms, especially shiitakes, are being studied for their ability to boost the immune system. Tossed with garlic and herbs, the mushrooms make a tasty, low-cal topper for a no-fuss pizza.

1   16-ounce loaf frozen bread dough, thawed
     Milk
6   cups sliced fresh mushrooms (such as shiitake, crimini, and/or oyster) (about 1 pound)
¼   cup snipped fresh herbs (such as oregano, basil, and/or parsley)
3   cloves garlic, minced
¼   cup olive oil
½   cup shredded provolone cheese (2 ounces)
¼   teaspoon coarse salt or salt

Grease a 15×10×1-inch baking pan; set aside. On a lightly floured surface, roll bread dough into a 15×10-inch rectangle. Transfer dough to the prepared pan. Prick dough generously with a fork. Let stand for 5 minutes. Brush with milk. Bake in a 425° oven about 10 minutes or until light brown. Cool on a wire rack about 5 minutes.

In a large bowl combine mushrooms, herbs, and garlic. Drizzle with olive oil; toss gently to coat. Sprinkle the cheese over baked crust. Top with mushroom mixture; sprinkle with salt.

Bake for 10 to 12 minutes more or until edges are golden brown and pizza is heated through. Makes 16 servings.

Nutrition information per serving: 121 cal., 5 g total fat (1 g sat. fat), 2 mg chol., 69 mg sodium, 13 g carbo., 4 g pro.

Mushroom Know-How

When shopping for fresh mushrooms, look for those that are firm, fresh, and plump with no bruising or moistness. If they're spotted or slimy, don't buy them.

Store mushrooms, unwashed, in the refrigerator up to 2 days. If they are prepackaged, store them in their original packaging. Don't store mushrooms in a closed plastic bag; mushrooms need to breathe. Store loose, unpackaged mushrooms in a paper bag or damp cloth bag in the refrigerator.

Stuffed Jalapeños

This recipe works equally well with fresh Anaheim peppers. For best results, choose Anaheims that are long and skinny.

½	of an 8-ounce tub cream cheese
2	tablespoons finely chopped green onion
2	tablespoons chopped pimiento, drained
1	clove garlic, minced
12	fresh jalapeño peppers or 2 to 3 fresh Anaheim peppers, halved lengthwise and seeded

In a small bowl stir together cream cheese, green onion, pimiento, and garlic. Spoon the cheese mixture into the jalapeño or Anaheim pepper halves. Cover and chill until serving time.

Before serving, cut the Anaheim-stuffed peppers into 2-inch bite-size pieces. Makes 12 appetizers.

Nutrition information per appetizer: 42 cal., 3 g total fat (2 g sat. fat), 10 mg chol., 35 mg sodium, 2 g carbo., 1 g pro.

Zesty Italian Peasant Bread

When you need a super-simple snack, it's hard to beat this bread, which also works well as an accompaniment to soup or as a side dish with grilled or broiled steaks and chops.

1	12-inch Italian bread shell (Boboli)
1	tablespoon olive oil or cooking oil
1	clove garlic, minced
⅛	teaspoon pepper
1	medium tomato, peeled, seeded, and chopped
⅓	cup crumbled Gorgonzola, blue, or feta cheese
1	tablespoon snipped fresh rosemary, oregano, or basil or 1 teaspoon dried rosemary, oregano, or basil, crushed
	Fresh rosemary, oregano, or basil sprigs (optional)

Lightly grease a baking sheet. Place bread shell on the prepared baking sheet. In a small bowl stir together oil, garlic, and pepper. Brush over bread shell. Sprinkle with tomato, crumbled cheese, and snipped fresh or dried herb.

Bake in a 400° oven for 10 to 15 minutes or until bread is heated through and cheese is slightly softened. Cut bread into 12 wedges. If desired, garnish with fresh herb sprigs. Serve hot. Makes 12 servings.

Nutrition information per serving: 126 cal., 5 g total fat (1 g sat. fat), 4 mg chol., 260 mg sodium, 17 g carbo., 5 g pro.

Spinach-Cheese Tart

The use of oil rather than shortening or butter in the pastry dough keeps saturated fat low. Try a fruity olive oil for added flavor.

Oil Pastry
2 eggs
1 cup light ricotta cheese
½ cup crumbled semisoft goat cheese (chèvre)
¼ cup fat-free milk
½ cup chopped spinach
¼ cup chopped, well drained, bottled roasted red sweet peppers
2 teaspoons snipped fresh oregano or ¾ teaspoon dried oregano, crushed
  Red and/or yellow sweet pepper strips (optional)
  Fresh oregano sprigs (optional)

Prepare Oil Pastry. On a lightly floured surface, roll pastry into a 12-inch circle. Ease into a 9½- or 10-inch tart pan with a removable bottom, being careful not to stretch the pastry. Trim pastry even with rim of pan. Do not prick.

Line pastry with a double thickness of foil. Bake in a 450° oven for 10 to 12 minutes or until edge is golden brown. Remove from oven. Remove foil. Reduce oven temperature to 325°.

Meanwhile, in a medium mixing bowl beat eggs slightly with an electric mixer. Add ricotta cheese, goat cheese, and milk; beat until smooth. Stir in spinach, roasted red peppers, and the snipped fresh or dried oregano. Pour egg mixture into tart shell.

Bake in the 325° oven about 20 minutes or until a knife inserted near the center comes out clean.

Let stand about 5 minutes before serving. If desired, top with sweet pepper strips and fresh oregano sprigs. Makes 12 servings.

Oil Pastry: In a medium bowl stir together 1¼ cups all-purpose flour and ¼ teaspoon salt. In a 1-cup measure combine ¼ cup fat-free milk and 3 tablespoons cooking oil. Add all at once to the flour mixture. Stir with a fork until dough forms a ball.

Nutrition information per serving: 142 cal., 7 g total fat (3 g sat. fat), 46 mg chol., 112 mg sodium, 12 g carbo., 6 g pro.

Baked Vegetable Dippers

Seasoned cornflake crumbs add crunch to these baked vegetables. Use warm pizza sauce as a dip.

Nonstick cooking spray
¾ cup cornflake crumbs
2 tablespoons grated Romano or
    Parmesan cheese
⅛ teaspoon garlic powder
⅛ teaspoon ground red pepper
2 egg whites
2 tablespoons water
2 small zucchini or yellow summer
    squash, cut into ¼-inch slices
1 cup cauliflower florets
1 cup halved small fresh mushrooms
    or broccoli florets
1 8-ounce can pizza sauce
Fresh oregano sprigs (optional)

Coat a large baking sheet with cooking spray; set aside.

In a small bowl combine cornflake crumbs, Romano or Parmesan cheese, garlic powder, and red pepper. In a small mixing bowl beat together the egg whites and water.

Dip squash, cauliflower, and mushrooms or broccoli into the egg white mixture and roll in the crumb mixture to coat. Place vegetables in a single layer on the prepared baking sheet. Bake in a 400° oven for 8 to 10 minutes or until coating is golden brown.

Meanwhile, in a small saucepan cook and stir pizza sauce over low heat until heated through. (Or place sauce in a microwave-safe bowl and microwave on 100% power [high] for 45 to 60 seconds.) Serve warm vegetables with pizza sauce for dipping. If desired, garnish with oregano. Makes 8 servings.

Nutrition information per serving: 51 cal., 1 g total fat (0 g sat. fat), 1 mg chol., 232 mg sodium, 9 g carbo., 3 g pro.

Fizzy Mint-Chocolate Soda

Sipping one of these ice cream quenchers in your backyard is one of summer's simple pleasures. These old-fashioned favorites are bound to lure the neighbors.

¼	cup chocolate-flavored syrup
1	pint (2 cups) mint-chocolate chip ice cream
2	cups carbonated water or cream soda, chilled

Pour 1 teaspoon of the chocolate syrup into the bottom of each of 4 tall glasses. Add 1 scoop (¼ cup) of the ice cream to each glass.

Add 2 more teaspoons of chocolate syrup to each glass. Top with another scoop of ice cream. Slowly pour carbonated water or cream soda into glasses. Makes 4 servings.

Nutrition information per serving: 245 cal., 11 g total fat (6 g sat. fat), 26 mg chol., 84 mg sodium, 33 g carbo., 4 g pro.

Spiced Fruit Punch

To serve this punch without alcohol, substitute two 1-liter bottles of chilled club soda or carbonated water for the wine.

½	cup water
⅓	cup sugar
12	inches stick cinnamon, broken
½	teaspoon whole cloves
4	cups apple juice or apple cider, chilled
1	12-ounce can apricot nectar, chilled
¼	cup lemon juice
2	750-milliliter bottles dry white wine, chilled

In a small saucepan combine water, sugar, stick cinnamon, and whole cloves. Bring to boiling; reduce heat. Cover and simmer for 10 minutes. Cover and chill for 2 to 24 hours.

Pour the sugar mixture through a fine-mesh sieve; discard spices. In a punch bowl combine the sugar mixture, apple juice or cider, apricot nectar, and lemon juice. Pour in wine. Makes 24 (4-ounce) servings.

Nutrition information per serving: 81 cal., 0 g total fat (0 g sat. fat), 0 mg chol., 5 mg sodium, 10 g carbo., 0 g pro.

Pick-Your-Fruit Smoothie

For the best flavor and texture, chill the juice well before preparing the smoothie.

2 cups strawberry juice blend or strawberry drink, chilled

2 cups fresh or frozen unsweetened strawberries

1 8-ounce carton plain yogurt

2 to 4 tablespoons sugar or honey

½ teaspoon vanilla

Toasted wheat germ with brown sugar and honey (optional)

In a blender container combine strawberry juice blend or strawberry drink, strawberries, yogurt, sugar or honey, and vanilla. Cover and blend until nearly smooth, with small chunks of strawberry visible.

Divide the strawberry mixture among 4 glasses. If desired, sprinkle with wheat germ. Makes 4 servings.

Nutrition information per serving: 142 cal., 1 g total fat (1 g sat. fat), 3 mg chol., 53 mg sodium, 30 g carbo., 3 g pro.

Kiwi Smoothie: Prepare as above, except substitute kiwifruit juice blend for the strawberry juice blend and 1 cup peeled and cut-up kiwifruit for the strawberries.

Melon Smoothie: Prepare as above, except substitute orange or orange-tangerine juice for the strawberry juice blend and 1 cup cubed cantaloupe for the strawberries.

Raspberry Tea

Fruity Yogurt Sipper

Make this icy drink fruitier by substituting fruit-flavored yogurt for the vanilla yogurt.

1   ripe large banana or 2 medium
       peaches, peeled and pitted
1½ cups milk
1   8-ounce carton vanilla yogurt
1   to 2 tablespoons sifted powdered
       sugar
½   cup ice cubes

Cut fruit into chunks. In a blender container combine the fruit chunks, milk, vanilla yogurt, and powdered sugar. Cover and blend until smooth.

With blender running, add ice cubes, one at a time, through opening in lid. Blend until smooth. Makes 4 (8-ounce) servings.

Nutrition information per serving: 139 cal., 3 g total fat (2 g sat. fat), 10 mg chol., 79 mg sodium, 24 g carbo., 6 g pro.

Raspberry Tea

Take advantage of berry season by floating fresh raspberries in this iced tea.

2   cups fresh or frozen red raspberries
4   or 5 tea bags
5   cups boiling water
    Ice cubes
    Lime wedges (optional)
    Fresh red raspberries (optional)

In a large glass bowl place the 2 cups raspberries and the tea bags. Pour boiling water over raspberries and tea bags. Cover and let stand for 5 minutes. Remove tea bags; discard.

Pour the tea mixture through a wire strainer placed over a large glass measure or a pitcher; discard berries. Cool for several hours. If desired, chill. Serve the tea in tall glasses over ice cubes. If desired, garnish with lime slices and additional fresh raspberries. Makes 6 (about 6-ounce) servings.

Nutrition information per serving: 12 cal., 0 g total fat (0 g sat. fat), 0 mg chol., 6 mg sodium, 3 g carbo., 0 g pro.

Salads,
SOUPS & STEWS

Contents

Beef and Three-Cheese Tortellini Salad

Cheese-filled pasta, cubes of Colby or cheddar, and grated Parmesan make up the trio of cheeses in this make-ahead salad.

2 cups frozen or refrigerated cheese-filled tortellini (about 7 ounces)

8 ounces cooked lean beef or cooked lean ham, cut into thin strips (1½ cups)

1 cup cubed Colby or cheddar cheese (4 ounces)

1 cup broccoli florets

1 small yellow summer squash or zucchini, halved lengthwise and sliced (1 cup)

Creamy Parmesan Dressing

Curly endive or leaf lettuce

1 cup cherry tomatoes, halved

Cook tortellini according to package directions. Drain tortellini. Rinse with cold water; drain again.

In a large bowl combine tortellini, beef or ham strips, Colby or cheddar cheese, broccoli florets, and sliced yellow summer squash or zucchini. Pour Creamy Parmesan Dressing over beef mixture; toss gently to coat. Cover and chill for 4 to 24 hours.

To serve, line dinner plates with curly endive or leaf lettuce. Divide the beef mixture among plates. Top the salads with cherry tomatoes. Makes 4 servings.

Creamy Parmesan Dressing: In a small bowl combine ½ cup mayonnaise or salad dressing; 2 tablespoons grated Parmesan cheese; 1 tablespoon snipped fresh marjoram or 1 teaspoon dried marjoram, crushed; 1 tablespoon red wine vinegar; and ¼ teaspoon pepper.

Nutrition information per serving: 593 cal., 39 g total fat (11 g sat. fat), 111 mg chol., 641 mg sodium, 32 g carbo., 31 g pro.

Hearty Beef Salad with Horseradish Dressing

If the weather's right, you can grill the sirloin steak for this tasty salad. Place the meat on the rack of an uncovered grill directly over medium coals. Grill for 14 to 18 minutes for medium rare (145°) or 18 to 22 minutes for medium (160°).

8	ounces green beans
1½	cups packaged, peeled baby carrots
12	ounces boneless beef top sirloin steak, cut 1 inch thick
4	cups torn Boston or Bibb lettuce
1	16-ounce can julienne beets, rinsed and drained
	Horseradish Dressing
	Cracked pepper (optional)

Wash green beans; remove ends and strings. Cut beans in half crosswise. In a covered medium saucepan cook the green beans in boiling water for 5 minutes. Add the baby carrots and cook for 10 to 15 minutes more or until vegetables are tender; drain. Cover and chill for 4 to 24 hours.

Trim fat from meat. Place meat on the unheated rack of a broiler pan. Broil 3 to 4 inches from the heat to desired doneness, turning once. [Allow 15 to 17 minutes for medium rare (145°) or 20 to 22 minutes for medium (160°).] Thinly slice across grain into bite-size strips.

Divide torn lettuce among dinner plates. Arrange green beans, baby carrots, meat slices, and beets on lettuce. Spoon the Horseradish Dressing over salads. If desired, sprinkle each salad with pepper. Makes 4 servings.

Horseradish Dressing: In a small bowl beat together one-half of a 3-ounce package cream cheese, softened, and 2 tablespoons horseradish sauce. Stir in enough milk (3 to 4 tablespoons) to make a dressing of drizzling consistency. Cover and chill until serving time. (Dressing will thicken slightly if made ahead and chilled.)

Nutrition information per serving: 360 cal., 15 g total fat (6 g sat. fat), 94 mg chol., 497 mg sodium, 24 g carbo., 32 g pro.

Flank Steak Salad with Pineapple Salsa

The fresh fruit salsa that enlivens this warm steak salad starts with green picante sauce. Just add pineapple, sweet pepper, and mandarin oranges and serve.

2   cups peeled, cored, and chopped fresh pineapple
1   11-ounce can mandarin orange sections, drained
½   cup chopped red and/or green sweet pepper
⅓   cup mild green picante sauce or green taco sauce
12 ounces beef flank steak or boneless beef sirloin steak, cut ½ to ¾ inch thick
½   teaspoon purchased Mexican seasoning or Homemade Mexican Seasoning (see recipe, page 211)
1   tablespoon olive oil
4   to 6 cups torn mixed salad greens

For pineapple salsa, in a medium bowl gently stir together pineapple, mandarin oranges, sweet pepper, and green picante sauce or taco sauce. Set aside.

Trim fat from meat. Thinly slice meat across the grain into bite-size strips. Sprinkle with Mexican seasoning or chili powder; toss to coat.

In a large skillet cook and stir half of the seasoned meat in hot oil over medium-high heat for 2 to 3 minutes or until meat is slightly pink in center. Remove from skillet. Repeat with the remaining meat.

Divide mixed greens among dinner plates. Top with meat strips and pineapple salsa. Makes 4 servings.

Nutrition information per serving: 245 cal., 10 g total fat (3 g sat. fat), 40 mg chol., 224 mg sodium, 23 g carbo., 18 g pro.

ℙREPARING PINEAPPLE

To peel and core a pineapple, first slice off the bottom stem end and the green top. Stand the pineapple on one cut end and slice off the skin in wide strips from top to bottom. Remove the eyes by cutting diagonally around the fruit, following the pattern of the eyes and making narrow wedge-shaped grooves. Cut away as little of the fruit as possible. Then slice or chop the fruit away from the core. Discard core.

Asian Pork-Cabbage Salad

Rice vinegars, known for their subtle tang and slightly sweet flavor, are used frequently in Oriental cooking. Made from rice wine or sake, they are usually clear to pale gold in color.

1   3-ounce package pork-flavored ramen noodles
¼   cup rice vinegar or white wine vinegar
2   tablespoons salad oil
1   tablespoon sugar
½   teaspoon toasted sesame oil
¼   teaspoon pepper
1   8¾-ounce can whole baby corn, drained
1   cup fresh pea pods or ½ of a 6-ounce package frozen pea pods, thawed
2   cups shredded cabbage
8   ounces cooked lean pork, cut into bite-size strips (1½ cups)
½   of a 14-ounce can straw mushrooms (1 cup) or one 6-ounce can whole mushrooms, drained
¼   cup sliced green onions
¼   cup sliced radishes
    Bok choy leaves
2   teaspoons sesame seeds, toasted

Cook ramen noodles according to package directions, omitting the seasoning package. Drain and set aside.

Meanwhile, for dressing, in a screw-top jar combine the seasoning package from the ramen noodles, the vinegar, salad oil, sugar, sesame oil, and pepper. Cover and shake well to dissolve seasonings.

Cut each ear of baby corn in half crosswise. If using fresh pea pods, trim ends and remove strings. In a large bowl combine cooked noodles, baby corn, pea pods, cabbage, pork, mushrooms, green onions, and radishes. Shake dressing well. Pour over cabbage mixture; toss gently to coat. Cover and chill for 4 to 24 hours.

Line dinner plates with bok choy leaves. Divide pork mixture among plates. Sprinkle each salad with sesame seeds. Makes 4 servings.

Nutrition information per serving: 386 cal., 20 g total fat (4 g sat. fat), 52 mg chol., 830 mg sodium, 31 g carbo., 23 g pro.

Chicken Salad with Raspberry Vinaigrette

If you like, arrange all the ingredients on a large glass salad plate and pass the dressing in a small cruet.

2 cups torn leaf lettuce
2 cups torn radicchio
2 cups torn arugula
1 medium Belgian endive, cut up
1 tablespoon Dijon-style mustard
1 tablespoon honey
¼ teaspoon salt
⅛ teaspoon pepper
4 medium skinless, boneless
    chicken breast halves (about
    1 pound total)
2 medium oranges, peeled and sliced
1 pink grapefruit, peeled and
    sectioned
1 avocado, halved, seeded, peeled,
    and sliced
2 green onions, thinly bias-sliced
    Raspberry Vinaigrette
    Fresh red raspberries (optional)

In a large bowl combine the leaf lettuce, radicchio, arugula, and Belgian endive; toss gently to mix. Cover and chill up to 2 hours. For sauce, in a small bowl combine the Dijon mustard, honey, salt, and pepper; set aside.

Place chicken on the rack of an uncovered grill directly over medium coals. Grill for 12 to 15 minutes or until no longer pink (170°), turning once and brushing with sauce the last 2 minutes of grilling. Cool chicken slightly; cut into thin strips.

Arrange the lettuce mixture on dinner plates. Arrange chicken strips, oranges, grapefruit sections, avocado slices, and green onions on lettuce mixture. Drizzle some of the Raspberry Vinaigrette over salads. If desired, garnish with fresh raspberries. Makes 4 servings.

Raspberry Vinaigrette: In a blender container combine one 10-ounce package frozen red raspberries, thawed; 2 tablespoons olive oil or salad oil; 2 tablespoons lemon juice; and 1 clove garlic, minced. Cover and blend until smooth. Press the berry mixture through a fine-mesh sieve; discard seeds. Cover and chill until serving time. Reserve any remaining dressing for another use.

Nutrition information per serving: 331 cal., 15 g total fat (1 g sat. fat), 59 mg chol., 295 mg sodium, 26 g carbo., 25 g pro.

Chicken Fajita Salad

You can make the Tortilla Cups up to five days ahead. Simply store them in an airtight container at room temperature.

4   small skinless, boneless chicken breast halves (about 12 ounces total)
½   cup bottled Italian salad dressing
½   cup bottled salsa
1   tablespoon salad oil
1   small yellow summer squash or zucchini, cut into thin bite-size strips (1 cup)
1   medium red sweet pepper, cut into thin bite-size strips (1 cup)
3   green onions, bias-sliced into 1-inch pieces (⅓ cup)
4   Tortilla Cups
    Dairy sour cream (optional)
    Frozen avocado dip, thawed (optional)
    Bottled salsa (optional)
½   cup shredded cheddar cheese (2 ounces)
4   cups shredded iceberg lettuce
1   cup chopped tomato

Cut chicken into thin bite-size strips; set aside. For marinade, in a large bowl combine Italian salad dressing and the ½ cup salsa. Add chicken strips; stir to coat. Cover and marinate in the refrigerator for 4 to 24 hours. Drain chicken, discarding marinade.

Add salad oil to a wok or large skillet. Preheat over medium-high heat (add more oil if necessary during cooking). Stir-fry yellow squash or zucchini in hot oil about 2 minutes or until crisp-tender. Remove squash from wok.

Add the sweet pepper and green onions to wok. Stir-fry for 2 to 3 minutes or until crisp-tender. Remove from wok. Add chicken to wok. Stir-fry for 2 to 3 minutes or until chicken is no longer pink. Remove from heat.

To serve, place Tortilla Cups on dinner plates. Divide chicken strips and vegetables among cups. If desired, top with sour cream, avocado dip, and/or additional salsa. Sprinkle with cheese. Arrange lettuce and tomato on plates alongside the cups. Makes 4 servings.

Tortilla Cups: Lightly brush one side of six 9- or 10-inch flour tortillas with a small amount of water or coat with nonstick cooking spray. Coat 6 small oven-proof bowls or 16-ounce individual casseroles with cooking spray. Press tortillas, coated sides up, into bowls. Place a ball of foil into each tortilla cup. Bake in a 350° oven for 15 to 20 minutes or until cups are light brown. Remove foil; cool cups on wire racks. Remove from bowls.

Nutrition information per serving: 389 cal., 23 g total fat (5 g sat. fat), 69 mg chol., 488 mg sodium, 23 g carbo., 24 g pro.

Tarragon Turkey Salad with Wild Rice

Often teamed with turkey or chicken, aromatic tarragon has an aniselike flavor with undertones of sage.

⅓ cup uncooked wild rice
1 14-ounce can chicken broth
⅓ cup uncooked long grain rice
2½ cups chopped cooked turkey or chicken (12 ounces)
½ cup bias-sliced celery
¼ cup sliced green onions
¼ cup olive oil or salad oil
2 tablespoons snipped fresh tarragon or 1 teaspoon dried tarragon, crushed
2 tablespoons white wine tarragon vinegar
2 tablespoons water
1 teaspoon Dijon-style mustard
¼ teaspoon salt
¼ teaspoon cracked black pepper
1 cup chopped apple
   Red-tipped leaf lettuce
1 large apple, sliced (optional)

Rinse wild rice in a strainer under cold running water about 1 minute. In a medium saucepan combine wild rice and chicken broth. Bring to boiling; reduce heat. Cover and simmer for 20 minutes.

Stir in the long grain rice. Return to boiling; reduce heat. Cover and simmer about 20 minutes more or until wild rice and long grain rice are tender and liquid is absorbed. Cool about 10 minutes.

In a large bowl combine the warm rice, turkey or chicken, celery, and green onions.

For dressing, in a screw-top jar combine olive oil or salad oil, tarragon, vinegar, water, mustard, salt, and pepper. Cover and shake well. Pour dressing over rice mixture; toss gently to coat. Cover and chill for 2 to 24 hours.

To serve, stir chopped apple into the rice mixture. Line dinner plates with leaf lettuce. Divide the rice mixture among lettuce-lined plates. If desired, garnish with apple slices. Makes 4 servings.

Nutrition information per serving: 443 cal., 22 g total fat (4 g sat. fat), 85 mg chol., 599 mg sodium, 29 g carbo., 33 g pro.

Blackened Fish Salad

Aromatic grilled herb bread makes a perfect partner for this crisp and hearty Cajun-style salad.

1 pound fresh or frozen catfish, cod, pollack, red snapper, or haddock fillets, ½ to ¾ inch thick

3 cups torn red-tipped leaf lettuce or leaf lettuce

3 cups torn spinach

2 medium oranges, peeled and sectioned

1 cup thinly sliced cucumber

1 small red sweet pepper, cut into thin bite-size strips (½ cup)

3 tablespoons snipped fresh basil or 1 teaspoon dried basil, crushed

1½ teaspoons snipped fresh thyme or ½ teaspoon dried thyme, crushed

1 teaspoon onion powder

1 teaspoon ground red pepper

1 teaspoon snipped fresh sage or ¼ teaspoon ground sage

½ teaspoon garlic salt

½ teaspoon white pepper

½ teaspoon black pepper

¼ cup margarine or butter, melted

⅔ cup Zesty Buttermilk Dressing

Thaw fish, if frozen. In a large salad bowl combine leaf lettuce, spinach, orange sections, cucumber slices, and pepper strips. Divide the lettuce mixture among dinner plates. Set aside.

In a small bowl combine basil, thyme, onion powder, ground red pepper, sage, garlic salt, white pepper, and black pepper. Rinse fish; pat dry with paper towels. Cut into 4 serving-size portions. Brush both sides of fish with some of the melted margarine or butter. Coat both sides with basil mixture.

Remove the rack from a charcoal grill. Place an unoiled 12-inch cast-iron skillet directly on hot coals. (If using a gas grill, place skillet on grill rack; turn heat to high.) Do not position handle over coals. Heat skillet about 5 minutes or until a drop of water sizzles.

Add fish to skillet. Carefully drizzle 2 teaspoons of the melted margarine or butter over fish. Grill for 2½ to 3 minutes or until fish is blackened. Turn fish; drizzle another 2 teaspoons melted margarine or butter over fish. Grill for 2½ to 3 minutes more or until blackened and fish flakes easily with a fork. Arrange fish on top of lettuce mixture. Serve with Zesty Buttermilk Dressing. Makes 4 servings.

Zesty Buttermilk Dressing: In a small bowl stir together ⅔ cup mayonnaise or salad dressing; ½ cup buttermilk; 1 tablespoon snipped fresh basil or 1 teaspoon dried basil, crushed; 1 tablespoon snipped fresh parsley; ½ teaspoon seasoned salt; ¼ teaspoon garlic powder; ¼ teaspoon onion powder; and ¼ teaspoon black pepper. Makes about 1¼ cups.

Nutrition information per serving: 247 cal., 14 g total fat (3 g sat. fat), 46 mg chol., 594 mg sodium, 11 g carbo., 22 g pro.

Oriental Spinach Tuna Salad

With both spinach and tuna rich in antioxidants, this salad packs a nutritious, low-fat punch.

1   9¼-ounce can chunk white tuna
        (water pack), chilled and drained
1   8-ounce can sliced water chestnuts
1   cup canned bean sprouts
6   cups torn spinach
1   large tomato, cut into wedges
1   stalk celery, chopped
1   green onion, sliced
3   tablespoons soy sauce
2   tablespoons rice vinegar
2   to 3 teaspoons toasted sesame oil
1   teaspoon sugar
⅛   teaspoon dry mustard
    Several dashes bottled hot
        pepper sauce

Break tuna into large chunks. Rinse and drain water chestnuts and bean sprouts. In a large salad bowl combine tuna, water chestnuts, bean sprouts, spinach, tomato wedges, celery, and green onion; toss gently to mix.

For dressing, in a screw-top jar combine soy sauce, rice vinegar, sesame oil, sugar, dry mustard, hot pepper sauce, and 1 tablespoon water. Cover and shake well.

Pour the dressing over the spinach mixture; toss gently to coat. Makes 4 servings.

Nutrition information per serving: 172 cal., 3 g total fat (1 g sat. fat), 12 mg chol., 1,095 mg sodium, 14 g carbo., 24 g pro.

Spanish-Style Shrimp and Rice Salad

For an authentic Spanish touch, line the serving plates with grape leaves instead of lettuce.

1   cup instant white rice
1   teaspoon instant chicken bouillon
        granules
¼   teaspoon ground turmeric
1   10-ounce package frozen peas
        with pearl onions
⅓   cup bottled Italian salad dressing
⅛   teaspoon ground red pepper
2   6-ounce packages frozen peeled,
        cooked shrimp, thawed
    Leaf lettuce

In a small saucepan bring 1 cup water to boiling. Stir in instant rice, chicken bouillon granules, and turmeric. Remove from heat. Cover and let stand for 5 minutes.

Meanwhile, cook peas with onions according to package directions. Drain. In a large bowl stir together rice mixture, peas with onions, salad dressing, and ground red pepper. Add shrimp; toss gently to coat. Cover and chill for several hours.

To serve, line dinner plates with lettuce. Divide the shrimp mixture among lettuce-lined plates. Makes 4 servings.

Nutrition information per serving: 283 cal., 10 g total fat (2 g sat. fat), 131 mg chol., 550 mg sodium, 28 g carbo., 18 g pro.

Tropical Scallop Salad

Sea scallops are larger than both bay and calico scallops. Cut any of the large scallops in half so they will cook evenly.

1 pound fresh or frozen sea scallops
1 15¼-ounce can pineapple spears (juice pack)
2 tablespoons white wine vinegar
1½ teaspoons sugar
¼ teaspoon finely shredded lime peel
1½ teaspoons lime juice
1 teaspoon cornstarch
⅛ teaspoon ground cinnamon
⅛ teaspoon ground cumin
1 cup fresh sugar snap peas
1 medium head Boston or Bibb lettuce
1 medium mango, seeded, peeled, and sliced
½ of a medium carrot, finely shredded

Thaw scallops, if frozen. Set aside.

For dressing, drain pineapple, reserving ⅓ cup of the juice. In a small saucepan combine the reserved pineapple juice, the white wine vinegar, sugar, lime peel, lime juice, cornstarch, cinnamon, and cumin. Cook and stir over medium heat until thickened and bubbly. Cook and stir for 2 minutes more. Remove from heat; cool.

In a small saucepan cook sugar snap peas in a small amount of boiling water for 1 minute. Drain and cool.

Rinse scallops; pat dry with paper towels. Cut any large scallops in half. Cook scallops in boiling, lightly salted water for 1 to 3 minutes or until scallops turn opaque. Drain.

Line dinner plates with lettuce leaves. Arrange scallops on one side of each plate. Starting from scallops, fan out pineapple spears, mango slices, and sugar snap peas on other side of each plate. Drizzle the dressing over salads. Sprinkle with carrot. Makes 4 servings.

Nutrition information per serving: *221 cal., 1 g total fat (0 g sat. fat), 34 mg chol., 178 mg sodium, 39 g carbo., 17 g pro.*

Egg Salad with Fresh Veggies

This colorful salad tastes great alone or in a sandwich. For the latter, split two small pita bread rounds and line them with lettuce leaves. Each pita holds about ½ cup of the egg mixture.

8 hard-cooked eggs (see note, page 207), chopped

1 small zucchini, quartered lengthwise and sliced (1 cup)

½ cup chopped celery

½ cup shredded carrot

2 tablespoons finely chopped green onion

2 tablespoons diced pimiento

⅓ cup mayonnaise or salad dressing

2 tablespoons bottled creamy Italian or cucumber salad dressing

1 tablespoon snipped fresh dill or 1 teaspoon dried dill

1 teaspoon prepared mustard

⅛ teaspoon salt
   Boston or Bibb lettuce leaves

1 to 2 tablespoons milk (optional)
   Fresh dill sprigs (optional)

In a medium bowl combine hard-cooked eggs, zucchini, celery, carrot, green onion, and pimiento. Stir in mayonnaise or salad dressing, Italian or cucumber salad dressing, snipped fresh or dried dill, mustard, and salt. Cover and chill for 4 to 24 hours.

To serve, line dinner plates with lettuce leaves. Stir egg mixture gently. If necessary, stir in enough of the milk to moisten. Divide the egg mixture among the lettuce-lined plates. If desired, garnish with additional fresh dill. Makes 4 servings.

Nutrition information per serving: 335 cal., 28 g total fat (6 g sat. fat), 437 mg chol., 399 mg sodium, 7 g carbo., 14 g pro.

Super Salad Pizza

Choose the greens of your liking: spinach, romaine lettuce, radicchio, arugula, watercress, Bibb lettuce, or Boston lettuce.

½ of a 17.3-ounce package (1 sheet) frozen puff pastry sheets, thawed
3 cups torn mixed salad greens
½ of a 9-ounce package frozen artichoke hearts, thawed, drained, and quartered
6 cherry tomatoes, halved
1 5-ounce container semisoft cheese with garlic and herbs or ½ of an 8-ounce tub cream cheese with chives and onion
2 teaspoons Dijon-style mustard
1 to 2 tablespoons milk
2 cups shredded mozzarella cheese (8 ounces)
½ of a medium avocado, peeled and sliced

On a lightly floured surface, roll pastry into a 12-inch square; cut into a 12-inch circle. Place on a 12-inch pizza pan or large baking sheet; build up edge of pastry. Generously prick the pastry with a fork. Bake in a 375° oven for 15 to 18 minutes or until golden brown (pastry will shrink). Cool.

Meanwhile, in a large bowl combine the salad greens, artichoke hearts, and cherry tomatoes.

For dressing, in a small bowl stir together the semisoft or cream cheese and mustard. Stir in enough of the milk to make a dressing of drizzling consistency. Drizzle half of the dressing over the greens mixture; toss gently to coat.

Sprinkle 1½ cups of the mozzarella cheese evenly over the crust. Broil about 3 inches from the heat for 1 to 1½ minutes or until cheese is melted. Spoon greens mixture on top of the melted cheese. Sprinkle with the remaining mozzarella cheese. Broil for 1 to 2 minutes more or until cheese is melted.

Arrange avocado slices on top of pizza. Cut into wedges. Serve immediately with the remaining dressing. Makes 6 servings.

Nutrition information per serving: 389 cal., 28 g total fat (8 g sat. fat), 42 mg chol., 462 mg sodium, 21 g carbo., 14 g pro.

Garbanzo Bean Salad

Garbanzo Bean Salad

Garbanzo beans, also known as chickpeas, have an irregular rounded shape, a nutty taste, and a firm texture.

1	6-ounce jar marinated artichoke hearts
2	tablespoons white wine vinegar
1	tablespoon salad oil
1½	teaspoons snipped fresh oregano or ½ teaspoon dried oregano, crushed
¾	teaspoon dry mustard
1	clove garlic, minced
2	15-ounce cans garbanzo beans, rinsed and drained
1	medium zucchini, halved lengthwise and sliced (1¼ cups)
1	cup chopped red sweet pepper
1	cup cubed cheddar cheese (4 ounces)
½	cup sliced pitted ripe olives
	Leaf lettuce

Drain artichoke hearts, reserving marinade. Coarsely chop artichoke hearts; set aside.

For dressing, in a screw-top jar combine reserved artichoke marinade, vinegar, oil, oregano, mustard, and garlic. Cover; shake well. Set aside.

In a large bowl combine artichokes, garbanzo beans, zucchini, sweet pepper, cheddar cheese, and olives. Shake dressing well. Pour over bean mixture; toss gently to coat. Cover and chill for 2 to 24 hours, stirring occasionally.

To serve, line dinner plates with lettuce. Divide the bean mixture among the lettuce-lined plates. Makes 4 or 5 servings.

Nutrition information per serving: 466 cal., 22 g total fat (7 g sat. fat), 30 mg chol., 815 mg sodium, 56 g carbo., 19 g pro.

Tortellini-Pesto Salad with Tomatoes

Use either frozen or refrigerated tortellini for this extra-easy, extra-tasty salad.

2	cups frozen or refrigerated cheese-filled tortellini (about 7 ounces)
1	cup cubed mozzarella cheese (4 ounces)
1	cup coarsely chopped, seeded tomato
½	cup purchased pesto
¼	cup pine nuts or slivered almonds, toasted
	Leaf lettuce

Cook tortellini according to package directions; drain. Rinse with cold water; drain again. In a large bowl combine tortellini, cheese, and tomato. Pour pesto over tortellini mixture; toss gently to coat. Cover and chill for 2 to 4 hours.

Just before serving, stir in pine nuts or almonds. To serve, line dinner plates with lettuce. Divide the pasta mixture among the lettuce-lined plates. Makes 4 servings.

Nutrition information per serving: 360 cal., 15 g total fat (4 g sat. fat), 51 mg chol., 453 mg sodium, 37 g carbo., 21 g pro.

Steak Soup

Sometimes called minute steaks, beef cubed steaks are thin, usually tenderized pieces of meat. They're a good choice for this soup because they cook quickly.

2	4-ounce beef cubed steaks
¼	teaspoon garlic salt
⅛	teaspoon pepper
1	tablespoon cooking oil
1	medium onion, chopped
1	stalk celery, chopped
4	cups water
1	10-ounce package frozen mixed vegetables
1	tablespoon instant beef bouillon granules
1	tablespoon Worcestershire sauce
1	teaspoon dried basil, crushed
1	7½-ounce can tomatoes, cut up
½	cup cold water
⅓	cup all-purpose flour

Sprinkle meat with garlic salt and pepper. In a large saucepan cook meat in hot oil over medium-high heat about 3 minutes or until brown, turning once. Remove meat from saucepan, reserving drippings in pan. Cut meat into cubes; set aside.

In the same saucepan cook onion and celery in the reserved drippings over medium heat until tender. Stir in meat cubes, the 4 cups water, the frozen mixed vegetables, beef bouillon granules, Worcestershire sauce, and basil.

Bring to boiling; reduce heat. Cover and simmer about 5 minutes or until vegetables are crisp-tender. Stir in undrained tomatoes.

In a screw-top jar shake together the ½ cup water and the flour; stir into meat mixture. Cook and stir until thickened and bubbly. Cook and stir for 1 minute more. Makes 5 servings.

Nutrition information per serving: 177 cal., 5 g total fat (1 g sat. fat), 29 mg chol., 784 mg sodium, 18 g carbo., 14 g pro.

TOMATO SHORTCUTS

To quickly cut up canned tomatoes, leave them in the can and use kitchen shears or scissors to snip them into small pieces. When a recipe calls for using both the cut-up tomatoes and their juice, there's no need to drain the tomatoes.

Pork and Mushroom Stew

This hearty stew is sure to satisfy the biggest of appetites.

1   pound pork stew meat, cut into
      1-inch cubes
2   tablespoons margarine or butter
1   10½-ounce can condensed
      chicken broth
¼   cup dry white wine
3   tablespoons snipped fresh parsley
1   bay leaf
¾   teaspoon snipped fresh thyme or
      ¼ teaspoon dried thyme, crushed
¼   teaspoon garlic powder
⅛   teaspoon pepper
2   cups frozen small whole onions
1   10-ounce package frozen tiny
      whole carrots
1   4-ounce can whole mushrooms,
      drained
¾   cup cold water
¼   cup all-purpose flour
1   tablespoon lemon juice

In a large saucepan cook meat, half at a time, in hot margarine or butter until brown. Return all meat to saucepan. Stir in chicken broth, wine, parsley, bay leaf, thyme, garlic powder, and pepper. Bring to boiling; reduce heat. Cover and simmer for 40 minutes.

Stir in the frozen onions, frozen carrots, and mushrooms. Return to boiling; reduce heat. Cover and simmer about 15 minutes more or until vegetables are tender. Remove bay leaf.

In a screw-top jar shake together water and flour. Stir flour mixture and lemon juice into meat mixture. Cook and stir until thickened and bubbly. Cook and stir for 1 minute more. Makes 4 servings.

Nutrition information per serving: 361 cal., 18 g total fat (5 g sat. fat), 74 mg chol., 800 mg sodium, 20 g carbo., 26 g pro.

Ham and Bean Soup with Vegetables

Today's comfort food, ham and bean soup takes on a new look with the colorful addition of carrots, parsnips, and spinach.

1   cup dry navy beans
1¼ to 1½ pounds meaty smoked pork
      hocks or one 1- to 1½-pound
      meaty ham bone
1   cup chopped onion
½   cup sliced celery
1   tablespoon instant chicken
      bouillon granules
1   tablespoon snipped fresh parsley
1   tablespoon snipped fresh thyme or
      1 teaspoon dried thyme, crushed
¼   teaspoon pepper
2   cups chopped parsnips or rutabaga
1   cup sliced carrots
1   10-ounce package frozen chopped
      spinach, thawed and well drained

Rinse beans. In a Dutch oven combine beans and 5 cups cold water. Bring to boiling; reduce heat. Simmer, uncovered, for 2 minutes. Remove from heat. Cover and let stand for 1 hour. (Or place beans in water in Dutch oven. Cover and soak beans overnight.) Drain and rinse beans.

In the same Dutch oven combine beans, 5 cups fresh water, pork hocks or ham bone, onion, celery, bouillon granules, parsley, thyme, and pepper. Bring to boiling; reduce heat. Cover and simmer for 1¾ hours. Remove pork hocks or ham bone; set aside to cool.

Mash beans slightly. Stir parsnips or rutabaga and carrots into bean mixture. Return to boiling; reduce heat. Cover and simmer about 15 minutes or until vegetables are tender.

Meanwhile, cut meat off bones and coarsely chop. Discard bones. Stir the chopped meat and the spinach into vegetable mixture. Heat through. Makes 4 or 5 servings.

Nutrition information per serving: 347 cal., 3 g total fat (1 g sat. fat), 19 mg chol., 1,175 mg sodium, 60 g carbo., 23 g pro.

Lamb Stew with Mashed Sweet Potatoes

This spiced blend of lamb, vegetables, and fruits is incredibly delicious served over Mashed Sweet Potatoes.

2 pounds lamb stew meat, cut into 1-inch cubes
¼ teaspoon salt
¼ teaspoon pepper
2 tablespoons cooking oil
2 tablespoons all-purpose flour
2 14-ounce cans vegetable broth
1 12-ounce can apricot or mango nectar
2 inches stick cinnamon or ¼ teaspoon ground cinnamon
3 cloves garlic, minced
½ teaspoon ground cumin
½ teaspoon ground cardamom
⅛ teaspoon thread saffron, crushed
3 medium carrots, cut into ½-inch pieces (1½ cups)
1½ cups frozen small whole onions
1 cup dried apricots
1 cup dried pitted plums (prunes)
Mashed Sweet Potatoes or mashed potatoes (optional)
Fresh sage leaves (optional)

Sprinkle meat with salt and pepper. In a 4-quart Dutch oven cook meat, half at a time, in hot oil over medium-high heat until brown. Drain off fat. Return all meat to Dutch oven.

Sprinkle meat with flour, stirring to coat. Stir in vegetable broth, nectar, cinnamon, garlic, cumin, cardamom, and saffron. Bring to boiling; reduce heat. Cover and simmer about 1 hour or until meat is nearly tender.

Stir carrots, onions, dried apricots, and dried plums into meat mixture. Return to boiling; reduce heat. Cover and simmer about 30 minutes more or until meat and vegetables are tender. If using, remove stick cinnamon.

If desired, serve the meat mixture over Mashed Sweet Potatoes or mashed potatoes and garnish with fresh sage. Makes 6 servings.

Mashed Sweet Potatoes: Peel and quarter 2 pounds sweet potatoes. In a covered large saucepan cook sweet potatoes in a moderate amount of boiling, lightly salted water for 20 to 25 minutes or until tender; drain. Mash with a potato masher or beat with an electric mixer on low speed. Add ¼ cup margarine or butter, cut up, and ¼ cup plain yogurt; beat until smooth. If necessary, stir in a little milk to make potatoes of desired consistency.

Nutrition information per serving: 418 cal., 12 g total fat (3 g sat. fat), 96 mg chol., 773 mg sodium, 51 g carbo., 33 g pro.

Oriental Chicken-Noodle Soup

Give this soup even more of an Oriental flare by substituting four wonton skins cut into thin strips for the fine egg noodles.

2 14-ounce cans chicken broth
1 cup water
1 medium red sweet pepper, cut
    into ¾-inch pieces
½ cup chopped carrot
½ cup dried fine egg noodles
⅓ cup thinly sliced green onions
1 tablespoon soy sauce
1 teaspoon grated fresh ginger
⅛ teaspoon crushed red pepper
1 cup chopped cooked chicken
    or turkey
1 cup fresh pea pods, halved crosswise

In a large saucepan or Dutch oven combine broth, water, sweet pepper, carrot, noodles, green onions, soy sauce, ginger, and crushed red pepper. Bring to boiling; reduce heat. Cover and simmer for 4 to 6 minutes or until vegetables are crisp-tender and noodles are tender.

Stir chicken or turkey and pea pods into broth mixture. Simmer, uncovered, for 1 to 2 minutes more or until pea pods are crisp-tender. Makes 3 or 4 servings.

Nutrition information per serving: 217 cal., 6 g total fat (2 g sat. fat), 53 mg chol., 1,343 mg sodium, 15 g carbo., 24 g pro.

Easy Cheesy Chicken Chowder

This hearty chowder lives up to its name. It's easy, it only takes about 20 minutes to cook, and with a whole cup of cheddar cheese, it's definitely cheesy!

1 cup small broccoli florets
1 cup frozen whole kernel corn
½ cup water
¼ cup chopped onion
½ teaspoon dried thyme, crushed
2 cups milk
1½ cups chopped cooked chicken
1 10¾-ounce can condensed cream
    of potato soup
1 cup shredded cheddar cheese
    (4 ounces)
    Dash pepper

In a large saucepan combine broccoli, corn, water, onion, and thyme. Bring to boiling; reduce heat. Cover and simmer for 8 to 10 minutes or until vegetables are tender. Do not drain.

Stir milk, chicken, potato soup, ¾ cup of the cheddar cheese, and the pepper into vegetable mixture. Cook and stir over medium heat until cheese is melted and mixture is heated through. Sprinkle with the remaining cheese. Makes 4 servings.

Nutrition information per serving: 380 cal., 18 g total fat (9 g sat. fat), 94 mg chol., 970 mg sodium, 25 g carbo., 31 g pro.

Oriental Chicken-Noodle Soup

Easy Mulligatawny Soup

This is a simplified version of the classic, curry-flavored Indian soup.

2½ cups chicken broth
1 cup chopped apples (2 small)
1 cup chopped carrots (2 medium)
1 cup water
1 7½-ounce can tomatoes, cut up
½ cup chopped celery (1 stalk)
⅓ cup uncooked long grain rice
¼ cup chopped onion
¼ cup raisins
1 tablespoon snipped fresh parsley
1 to 1½ teaspoons curry powder
1 teaspoon lemon juice
¼ teaspoon coarsely ground pepper
⅛ teaspoon ground mace or nutmeg
1½ cups chopped cooked chicken
       or turkey

In a large saucepan combine chicken broth, apples, carrots, water, undrained tomatoes, celery, uncooked rice, onion, raisins, parsley, curry powder, lemon juice, pepper, and mace or nutmeg.

Bring to boiling; reduce heat. Cover and simmer about 20 minutes or until rice is tender. Stir in the chopped chicken or turkey; heat through. Makes 4 servings.

Nutrition information per serving: 275 cal., 6 g total fat (2 g sat. fat), 51 mg chol., 677 mg sodium, 34 g carbo., 22 g pro.

QUICK-COOKED POULTRY

If your recipe calls for cooked poultry and you don't have any leftovers to use, purchase a deli-roasted chicken. A roasted chicken yields 1½ to 2 cups boneless chopped meat.

Another option is to poach chicken breasts. In a large skillet place 12 ounces skinless, boneless chicken breast halves and 1½ cups water. Bring to boiling; reduce heat. Cover and simmer for 12 to 14 minutes or until chicken is no longer pink (170°). Drain well. Cut up chicken as recipe directs. The 12 ounces of boneless breasts yield about 2 cups cubed, cooked chicken.

White Chili with Salsa Verde

This wintertime dish looks like navy bean soup and tastes like a mild-flavored chili. Unlike ordinary chili, however, it's topped with a spicy Mexican salsa that's made with tomatillos.

12   ounces uncooked ground turkey
½   cup chopped onion
1   clove garlic, minced
3   cups water
1   15-ounce can Great Northern or
     white kidney (cannellini) beans,
     rinsed and drained
1   4-ounce can diced green chile
     peppers
2   teaspoons instant chicken
     bouillon granules
1   teaspoon ground cumin
¼   teaspoon black pepper
¼   cup water
2   tablespoons all-purpose flour
1   cup shredded Monterey Jack cheese
     (4 ounces)
     Salsa Verde

In a large saucepan or Dutch oven cook ground turkey, onion, and garlic until turkey is brown. Drain off fat, if necessary. Stir in the 3 cups water, the beans, undrained chile peppers, chicken bouillon granules, cumin, and black pepper.

Bring to boiling; reduce heat. Cover and simmer for 30 minutes. Stir together the ¼ cup water and the flour; stir into bean mixture. Cook and stir until thickened and bubbly. Cook and stir for 1 minute more. Top each serving with cheese and Salsa Verde. Makes 4 servings.

Salsa Verde: In a medium bowl stir together 5 or 6 fresh tomatillos (6 to 8 ounces), husks removed and finely chopped, or one 13-ounce can tomatillos, rinsed, drained, and finely chopped; 2 tablespoons finely chopped onion; 2 fresh serrano or jalapeño peppers, seeded and finely chopped; 1 tablespoon snipped fresh cilantro or parsley; 1 teaspoon finely shredded lime peel; and ½ teaspoon sugar. Cover and chill up to 2 days or freeze; thaw before using.

Nutrition information per serving: 319 cal., 16 g total fat (7 g sat. fat), 57 mg chol., 927 mg sodium, 24 g carbo., 26 g pro.

Quick-to-Fix Turkey and Rice Soup

Turn your leftover Thanksgiving turkey into a meal your family will love.

4   cups chicken broth
1   cup water
1   teaspoon snipped fresh rosemary
    or ¼ teaspoon dried rosemary,
    crushed
¼   teaspoon pepper
1   10-ounce package frozen mixed
    vegetables
1   cup instant white rice
2   cups chopped cooked turkey
    or chicken
1   14½-ounce can tomatoes, cut up

In a large saucepan or Dutch oven combine broth, water, rosemary, and pepper. Bring to boiling. Stir in mixed vegetables and rice.

Return to boiling; reduce heat. Cover and simmer for 10 to 15 minutes or until vegetables and rice are tender. Stir in turkey or chicken and undrained tomatoes. Heat through. Makes 6 servings.

Nutrition information per serving: 209 cal., 4 g total fat (1 g sat. fat), 36 mg chol., 699 mg sodium, 24 g carbo., 20 g pro.

Seafood Chowder

Serve this quick soup with lefse (a very thin Scandinavian potato bread) or crusty French bread.

1 pound skinless, boneless sea bass,
   red snapper, and/or catfish fillets,
   ¾ inch thick
½ cup chopped onion
2 cloves garlic, minced
1 tablespoon butter or olive oil
4 cups water
1 tablespoon lemon juice
2 fish bouillon cubes
1 bay leaf
½ teaspoon instant chicken
   bouillon granules
½ teaspoon dried thyme, crushed
¼ teaspoon fennel seeds
   Dash powdered saffron (optional)
4 roma tomatoes, halved lengthwise
   and thinly sliced
   Fresh thyme sprigs (optional)

Rinse fish; pat dry with paper towels. Cut the fish into ¾-inch pieces. Set aside.

In a large saucepan cook onion and garlic in hot butter or olive oil over medium heat until tender. Stir in water, lemon juice, fish bouillon cubes, bay leaf, chicken bouillon granules, dried thyme, fennel, and, if desired, saffron. Bring to boiling, stirring occasionally.

Stir in fish and tomatoes. Return to boiling; reduce heat. Cover and simmer for 10 minutes. Discard bay leaf. If desired, garnish the chowder with fresh thyme sprigs. Makes 4 to 6 servings.

Nutrition information per serving: 160 cal., 5 g total fat (2 g sat. fat), 55 mg chol., 683 mg sodium, 6 g carbo., 22 g pro.

Fresh Tomato Soup with Tortellini

Quick Asian Fish Soup

Skimp on time, not taste, when you cook up this intriguing Oriental-inspired soup.

12 ounces fresh or frozen monkfish, cusk, cod, or croaker fillets, ½ inch thick
 1 10¾-ounce can condensed chicken with rice soup
1½ cups water
 2 tablespoons reduced-sodium soy sauce
 ⅛ teaspoon ground red pepper
1½ cups loose-pack frozen broccoli, red pepper, onions, and mushrooms
 1 tablespoon lemon juice

Thaw fish, if frozen. Rinse fish; pat dry with paper towels. Cut fish into ½-inch pieces. Set aside.

In a large saucepan combine soup, water, soy sauce, and ground red pepper. Bring to boiling. Stir in frozen vegetables. Return to boiling; reduce heat. Cover and simmer for 5 minutes. Stir in fish.

Cover and cook for 3 to 5 minutes more or until fish flakes easily with a fork. Stir in lemon juice. Makes 3 servings.

Nutrition information per serving: 155 cal., 2 g total fat (1 g sat. fat), 48 mg chol., 1,152 mg sodium, 10 g carbo., 23 g pro.

Fresh Tomato Soup with Tortellini

Add your favorite brand of tortellini, a hat-shaped pasta filled with meat or cheese, to this fresh tomato-sage-flavored soup.

 1 cup chopped onion
 1 tablespoon olive oil or cooking oil
 2 pounds ripe tomatoes (6 medium), peeled, seeded, and cut up
1½ cups reduced-sodium chicken broth
1½ cups water
 1 8-ounce can low-sodium tomato sauce
 1 tablespoon snipped fresh sage or 1 teaspoon dried sage, crushed
 ¼ teaspoon salt
 ¼ teaspoon pepper
 4 ounces dried tortellini
    Fresh sage sprigs (optional)
 ¼ cup finely shredded Parmesan cheese

In a large saucepan or Dutch oven cook onion in hot oil until tender. Stir in tomatoes, chicken broth, water, tomato sauce, snipped fresh or dried sage, salt, and pepper. Bring to boiling; reduce heat. Cover and simmer for 30 minutes. Remove from heat; cool slightly. Meanwhile, cook tortellini according to package directions; drain.

Press the tomato mixture through a food mill. (Or place one-third to one-half of the mixture at a time in a blender container or food processor bowl. Cover and blend or process until smooth.) Return tomato mixture to saucepan. Stir in cooked tortellini; heat through. If desired, garnish each serving with fresh sage sprigs. Pass the Parmesan cheese. Makes 4 servings.

Nutrition information per serving: 266 cal., 9 g total fat (2 g sat. fat), 5 mg chol., 744 mg sodium, 35 g carbo., 12 g pro.

Beef & PORK

Contents

Grilled Rump Roast with Curried Mustard

A mixture of mustard, honey, curry powder, and chives makes a glistening glaze for the roast. Stir more of the same mustard mixture into sour cream for a refreshing sauce.

1   **3-pound boneless beef round rump roast**
2   **tablespoons Dijon-style mustard**
1   **tablespoon honey**
1   **teaspoon curry powder**
1   **teaspoon snipped fresh chives**
½   **cup dairy sour cream**
    Snipped fresh chives (optional)

Trim fat from meat. In a small bowl stir together mustard, honey, curry powder, and the 1 teaspoon chives. Remove about 1 tablespoon of the mustard mixture; brush over meat. Insert an oven-going meat thermometer into center of meat.

For sauce, in a small bowl combine the remaining mustard mixture and the sour cream. Cover and chill until serving time.

In a covered grill arrange medium coals around a drip pan. Test for medium-low heat above the pan. Place meat on grill rack over drip pan. Cover and grill to desired doneness. [Allow 1¼ to 1¾ hours for medium rare (140°) or 1¾ to 2¼ hours for medium (155°).]

Remove meat from grill and cover with foil. Let stand for 15 minutes before slicing. (The meat's temperature will rise 5° during standing.)

Serve the meat with sauce and, if desired, additional snipped chives. Makes 12 servings.

Nutrition information per serving: 202 cal., 9 g total fat (4 g sat. fat), 81 mg chol., 108 mg sodium, 2 g carbo., 26 g pro.

Weeknight Steak with Vegetables

Sautéeing the vegetables gives them a robust flavor and keeps most of the work for this dish in one pan.

2 tablespoons olive oil
2 medium zucchini and/or yellow
    summer squash, cut into
    1-inch chunks
2 stalks celery, cut into 1-inch slices
1 large onion, cut into thick wedges
3 cloves garlic, peeled
1 teaspoon dried rosemary, crushed
1 pound boneless beef top sirloin
    steak, cut ¾ inch thick
½ cup Zinfandel or other fruity dry
    red wine
1 14½-ounce can diced tomatoes
    with basil, oregano, and garlic

In a large skillet heat 1 tablespoon of the oil over medium heat. Cook the squash, celery, onion, garlic, and rosemary in the hot oil for 6 to 7 minutes or just until vegetables are crisp-tender, stirring occasionally. Remove from skillet.

Trim fat from steak. Cut steak into 4 serving-size portions. Add remaining oil to skillet. Add steak to hot skillet; sprinkle with salt and pepper. Cook over medium-high heat for 4 to 5 minutes or until medium rare (145°), turning once. Remove steak from skillet. Cover and keep warm.

Add the wine to skillet, scraping up any browned bits on bottom. Stir in undrained tomatoes. Bring to boiling. Boil gently, uncovered, about 5 minutes or until slightly thickened. Return cooked vegetables to skillet. Cook and stir just until heated through. Serve the vegetable mixture over steak. Makes 4 servings.

Nutrition information per serving: 388 cal., 23 g total fat (7 g sat. fat), 74 mg chol., 362 mg sodium, 16 g carbo., 24 g pro.

ℐSING A MEAT THERMOMETER

To ensure perfectly cooked meat, check for doneness with a meat thermometer. For thinner foods, such as steaks, burgers, and chops, insert an instant-read thermometer through the side of the meat to get an accurate reading. Do not leave this type of thermometer in the food while it is cooking.

BLT Steak

A loaf of crusty bread and a bottle of red wine complete this bistro-style dinner.

2   12-ounce boneless beef top loin
    steaks, cut 1¼ inches thick
2   slices bacon, cut into quarters
½   cup bottled balsamic vinaigrette
    salad dressing
12 thin slices red and/or yellow
    tomatoes
2   cups mixed baby salad greens
    Fresh Italian flat-leaf parsley sprigs
    (optional)

Trim fat from steaks. Place steaks on the rack of an uncovered grill directly over medium coals. Grill to desired doneness, turning once. [Allow 13 to 15 minutes for medium rare (145°) or 16 to 18 minutes for medium (160°).]

Meanwhile, in a large skillet cook bacon pieces over medium heat until crisp. Drain bacon, reserving 1 tablespoon drippings in skillet. Add the balsamic vinaigrette dressing to reserved drippings in skillet. Cook and stir over high heat for 1 minute, scraping up any browned bits on bottom of skillet.

To serve, cut each steak in half. Arrange the steak portions on dinner plates. Top with tomato slices, bacon, mixed greens, and dressing from the skillet. If desired, garnish with parsley. Makes 4 servings.

Nutrition information per serving: *556 cal., 42 g total fat (14 g sat. fat), 122 mg chol., 636 mg sodium, 5 g carbo., 38 g pro.*

Italian-Style Pepper Steak

Enjoy this delicious steak in the summertime. For optimal flavor, use vine-ripened tomatoes and fresh herbs.

2 medium green and/or red sweet
   peppers, cut into thin strips
½ cup chopped onion (1 medium)
2 cloves garlic, minced
1 tablespoon cooking oil
12 ounces beef tenderloin or boneless
   top sirloin steak, cut ¾ inch thick
¾ cup beef broth
1½ teaspoons snipped fresh or
   ½ teaspoon dried herb (such as
   oregano, basil, or rosemary),
   crushed
2 medium tomatoes, seeded and
   chopped (1 cup)
   Fresh herb sprigs (optional)

In a large skillet cook sweet peppers, onion, and garlic in hot oil about 4 minutes or until vegetables are crisp-tender. Remove from skillet. Cover and keep warm.

Trim fat from steak. Cut steak into 4 serving-size portions. Add steak to skillet (add more oil if necessary during cooking). Sprinkle steak with salt. Cook over medium-high heat for 6 to 8 minutes or until medium (160°), turning once. Transfer to a serving platter, reserving drippings in skillet. Cover and keep warm.

Carefully add beef broth and snipped fresh or dried herb to reserved drippings in skillet. Bring to boiling. Boil gently, uncovered, over medium heat for 2 to 3 minutes or until broth is reduced to ⅓ cup, scraping up any browned bits on bottom. Remove from heat.

Stir the cooked vegetables and tomatoes into broth. Heat through. Serve the vegetable mixture over steak. If desired, garnish with fresh herb sprigs. Makes 4 servings.

Nutrition information per serving: 185 cal., 9 g total fat (3 g sat. fat), 48 mg chol., 223 mg sodium, 8 g carbo., 18 g pro.

Horseradish-Dill Beef Stroganoff

Follow this quick-prep method to make a classic Old World recipe. The horseradish-sour cream sauce is an imperial touch.

3	cups dried wide noodles
3	cups broccoli florets (12 ounces)
½	cup light dairy sour cream
1½	teaspoons prepared horseradish
½	teaspoon snipped fresh dill
1	pound beef ribeye steak
1	small onion, cut into ½-inch slices
1	clove garlic, minced
1	tablespoon cooking oil
4	teaspoons all-purpose flour
½	teaspoon pepper
1	14-ounce can beef broth
3	tablespoons tomato paste
1	teaspoon Worcestershire sauce

Cook noodles according to package directions, adding broccoli the last 5 minutes of cooking; drain. Cover and keep warm.

Meanwhile, for sauce, in a small bowl stir together the sour cream, horseradish, and dill. Cover and chill until serving time.

Trim fat from meat. Slice meat across the grain into bite-size strips. In a large skillet cook half of the meat, the onion, and garlic in hot oil over medium-high heat about 3 minutes or until meat is slightly pink in center. Remove from skillet. Repeat with the remaining meat. Return all meat mixture to skillet.

Sprinkle meat with flour and pepper; stir to coat. Stir in the beef broth, tomato paste, and Worcestershire sauce. Cook and stir until thickened and bubbly. Cook and stir for 1 minute more.

To serve, divide the noodle mixture among bowls or dinner plates. Spoon the meat mixture on top of noodle mixture. Spoon the sauce on top of meat mixture. Makes 4 servings.

Nutrition information per serving: 368 cal., 15 g total fat (5 g sat. fat), 81 mg chol., 454 mg sodium, 32 g carbo., 29 g pro.

Szechwan Beef Stir-Fry

To partially freeze the meat, place it in the freezer for about 20 minutes. If you're starting with frozen meat, thaw it until it's soft but still icy.

12 ounces boneless beef sirloin steak or top round steak
1 8¾-ounce can whole baby corn, drained
3 tablespoons dry sherry or dry white wine
3 tablespoons soy sauce
2 tablespoons water
2 tablespoons bottled hoisin sauce
2 teaspoons cornstarch
2 teaspoons grated fresh ginger
1 teaspoon sugar
2 cloves garlic, minced
½ teaspoon crushed red pepper
¼ teaspoon black pepper (optional)
1 tablespoon cooking oil
1 cup thinly sliced carrots (2 medium)
1 red sweet pepper, cut into 1-inch pieces (1 cup)
2 cups hot cooked rice
   Lime peel curls (optional)

Trim fat from meat. Partially freeze meat. Thinly slice across the grain into bite-size strips. Set aside. If desired, cut baby corn in half crosswise. Set aside.

For sauce, in a small bowl stir together sherry or wine, soy sauce, water, hoisin sauce, cornstarch, ginger, sugar, garlic, red pepper, and, if desired, black pepper. Set aside.

Add cooking oil to a wok or large skillet. Preheat over medium-high heat (add more oil if necessary during cooking). Stir-fry carrots in hot oil for 2 minutes. Add baby corn and sweet pepper. Stir-fry for 1 to 2 minutes more or until crisp-tender. Remove vegetables from wok.

Add meat to wok. Stir-fry for 2 to 3 minutes or until meat is slightly pink in center. Push meat from center of wok.

Stir sauce. Add sauce to center of wok. Cook and stir until thickened and bubbly. Return cooked vegetables to wok. Stir all ingredients together to coat. Cook and stir for 1 to 2 minutes more or until mixture is heated through. Serve immediately over hot cooked rice. If desired, garnish with lime peel. Makes 4 servings.

Nutrition information per serving: 363 cal., 11 g total fat (4 g sat. fat), 57 mg chol., 1,396 mg sodium, 36 g carbo., 25 g pro.

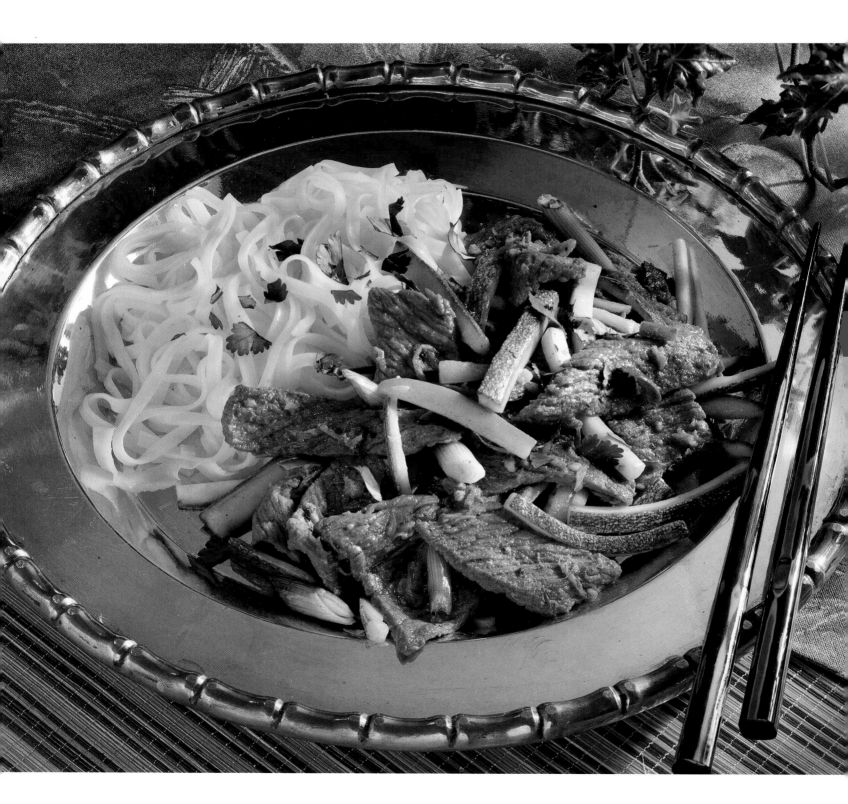

Spicy Thai Ginger Beef

Thai cooking is strongly influenced by both Chinese and Indian cuisines. In fact, the Thai people migrated from China's Yunnan province in the 13th century.

12 ounces beef top round steak
1 tablespoon fish sauce
1 tablespoon water
1 teaspoon finely shredded lime peel
1 tablespoon lime juice
1 teaspoon sugar
1 tablespoon cooking oil
2 medium zucchini, cut into thin bite-size strips (2 cups)
6 green onions, bias-sliced into 1-inch pieces (1 cup)
1 fresh, pickled, or canned jalapeño pepper, seeded and finely chopped
3 cloves garlic, minced
2 teaspoons grated fresh ginger
2 cups hot cooked rice sticks or rice
2 tablespoons snipped fresh cilantro

Trim fat from meat. Partially freeze meat. Thinly slice meat across the grain into bite-size strips. Set aside.

For sauce, in a small bowl stir together fish sauce, water, lime peel, lime juice, and sugar. Set aside.

Add cooking oil to a wok or large skillet. Preheat over medium-high heat (add more oil if necessary during cooking). Stir-fry zucchini in hot oil for 1 to 2 minutes or until crisp-tender. Remove zucchini from wok. Add green onions to wok. Stir-fry for 1½ minutes. Remove green onions from wok.

Add jalapeño pepper, garlic, and ginger to wok. Stir-fry for 15 seconds. Add meat. Stir-fry for 2 to 3 minutes or until meat is slightly pink in center. Return the cooked zucchini and green onions to wok.

Add sauce to center of wok. Cook and stir about 2 minutes or until heated through. Serve immediately with hot cooked rice sticks or rice. Sprinkle with cilantro. Makes 3 servings.

Nutrition information per serving: 339 cal., 10 g total fat (3 g sat. fat), 74 mg chol., 242 mg sodium, 30 g carbo., 31 g pro.

Beef Strips with Vermicelli

Strips of top round steak make a lean choice for this sauce whether you're counting calories or pennies.

8 ounces boneless beef top
   round steak
4 ounces dried vermicelli or spaghetti
1 tablespoon cooking oil
1 medium onion, chopped
1 14½-ounce can tomato wedges
1 9-ounce package frozen cut Italian-
   style green beans or green beans
1 4-ounce can sliced mushrooms,
   drained
½ of a 6-ounce can (⅓ cup) Italian-
   style tomato paste
½ teaspoon fennel seeds, crushed
   (optional)
¼ teaspoon pepper
1 tablespoon grated Parmesan cheese
   Grated Parmesan cheese (optional)

Trim fat from meat. Partially freeze meat. Thinly slice meat across the grain into bite-size strips. Cook pasta according to package directions; drain. Cover and keep warm.

Meanwhile, in a large skillet heat oil over medium-high heat. Add meat and onion. Cook and stir about 2 minutes or until meat is brown. Stir in undrained tomato wedges, green beans, mushrooms, tomato paste, fennel seeds (if desired), and pepper. Bring to boiling; reduce heat. Simmer, uncovered, for 7 to 8 minutes or until slightly thickened, stirring frequently. Stir in the 1 tablespoon cheese.

To serve, arrange pasta on dinner plates or a large platter. Spoon the meat mixture over pasta. If desired, sprinkle with additional Parmesan cheese. Makes 4 servings.

Nutrition information per serving: 278 cal., 7 g total fat (2 g sat. fat), 28 mg chol., 488 mg sodium, 38 g carbo., 18 g pro.

Marinated Steak Fajitas

It's easy to make tasty beef fajitas at home with this simple recipe. For extra flavor, top them with sour cream, chopped tomato, and fresh cilantro.

1   pound beef flank steak
3   tablespoons bottled chili sauce
2   tablespoons water
1   tablespoon Worcestershire sauce
1   teaspoon dried oregano, crushed
½   teaspoon chili powder
⅛   teaspoon garlic powder
⅛   teaspoon black pepper
10   7-inch flour tortillas
     Nonstick cooking spray
2   small red, yellow, and/or green
        sweet peppers, cut into thin
        bite-size strips
1   small onion, cut into thin wedges

Trim fat from meat. Thinly slice meat across the grain into bite-size strips. Place meat in a plastic bag set in a shallow dish. For marinade, in a small bowl stir together chili sauce, water, Worcestershire sauce, oregano, chili powder, garlic powder, and black pepper. Pour over meat; seal bag. Marinate in the refrigerator for 4 to 24 hours, turning bag occasionally.

Stack tortillas; wrap in foil. Bake in a 350° oven about 10 minutes or until warm. (Or just before serving, microwave tortillas, covered with a paper towel, on 100% power [high] about 1 minute.)

Coat a large nonstick skillet with cooking spray. Heat over medium-high heat. Add half of the meat mixture. Cook and stir for 2 to 3 minutes or until meat is slightly pink in center. Remove meat from skillet. Repeat with remaining meat mixture (add 1 teaspoon cooking oil if necessary). Remove meat from skillet, reserving juices in skillet.

Add the pepper strips and onion wedges to reserved juices in skillet. Bring to boiling; reduce heat. Cover and simmer for 3 to 4 minutes or until vegetables are crisp-tender. Stir the meat into vegetable mixture. Heat through.

To serve, place about ½ cup of the meat mixture on each tortilla. Roll up tortillas. Makes 5 servings.

Nutrition information per serving: 388 cal., 12 g total fat (4 g sat. fat), 43 mg chol., 541 mg sodium, 45 g carbo., 24 g pro.

Zippy Beef, Mac, and Cheese

Zippy Beef, Mac, and Cheese

Nothing goes better with this old favorite than a fresh side salad. Simply peel and section oranges and cut jicama into strips; arrange on a lettuce leaf and drizzle with an oil-and-vinegar dressing.

6 ounces dried elbow macaroni or corkscrew pasta (about 1½ cups)	In a 3-quart saucepan cook pasta according to package directions; drain. Meanwhile, in a large skillet cook ground meat until brown. Drain off fat.
12 ounces lean ground beef, lean ground pork, or uncooked ground turkey	
1 15-ounce can tomato sauce	Stir ground meat, tomato sauce, undrained tomatoes, American cheese, and chili powder into cooked pasta. Cook and stir over medium heat for 6 to 8 minutes or until heated through. Sprinkle each serving with Parmesan cheese. Makes 4 servings.
1 14½-ounce can stewed tomatoes or Mexican-style stewed tomatoes	
4 ounces American or sharp American cheese, cut into small pieces	
1 tablespoon chili powder	
Finely shredded or grated Parmesan cheese	

Nutrition information per serving: 342 cal., 15 g total fat (7 g sat. fat), 55 mg chol., 957 mg sodium, 32 g carbo., 20 g pro.

Easy Shepherd's Pie

Frozen mashed potatoes make quick work of this family-style ground meat- and soup-based skillet supper.

1 28-ounce package frozen mashed potatoes	Prepare the potatoes according to package directions using 4 cups of the frozen potatoes and the milk. Meanwhile, run cold water over frozen vegetables to separate. In a large skillet cook ground meat until brown. Drain off any fat. Stir in mixed vegetables, water, and onion.
1¾ cups milk	
1 10-ounce package frozen mixed vegetables	
1 pound lean ground beef, uncooked ground turkey, or uncooked ground chicken	Bring to boiling; reduce heat. Cover and simmer for 5 to 10 minutes or until vegetables are tender. Stir in soup, Worcestershire sauce, and thyme. Return to boiling. Drop potatoes in mounds on top of hot mixture. Sprinkle with cheese; reduce heat. Cover and simmer about 5 minutes or until heated through. Makes 6 servings.
¼ cup water	
1 teaspoon dried minced onion	
1 10¾-ounce can condensed tomato soup	
1 teaspoon Worcestershire sauce	
¼ teaspoon dried thyme, crushed	
½ cup shredded cheddar cheese	

Nutrition information per serving: 342 cal., 16 g total fat (7 g sat. fat), 62 mg chol., 541 mg sodium, 30 g carbo., 19 g pro.

Pepper-Bacon Burgers

The All-American burger gets a spicy makeover with the addition of serrano or jalapeño peppers.

1   beaten egg
¼   cup fine dry bread crumbs
6   slices crisp-cooked bacon, crumbled
4   to 6 fresh serrano peppers or 2 to
      3 fresh jalapeño peppers, seeded and
      finely chopped (3 tablespoons)
2   tablespoons milk
1   pound lean ground beef
1   fresh Anaheim pepper or mild green
      chile pepper, seeded and sliced
1   small onion, thinly sliced and
      separated into rings
2   tablespoons margarine or butter
4   kaiser rolls or hamburger buns,
      split and toasted
4   lettuce leaves (optional)

In a large bowl combine egg, bread crumbs, bacon, serrano or jalapeño peppers, and milk. Add ground beef; mix well. Form into four ¾-inch-thick patties.

Place patties on the rack of an uncovered grill directly over medium coals. Grill for 14 to 18 minutes or until done (160°), turning once.

Meanwhile, in a small saucepan cook the Anaheim or green chile pepper and onion in hot margarine or butter about 10 minutes or until onion is tender.

If desired, line bottoms of rolls or buns with lettuce. Top with burgers and onion mixture. Replace roll or bun tops. Makes 4 servings.

Nutrition information per serving: 550 cal., 29 g total fat (9 g sat. fat), 132 mg chol., 733 mg sodium, 38 g carbo., 32 g pro.

Meatballs in Pasta Nests

These tiny meatballs, inspired by the Italian classic osso buco, tuck into a bed of pasta. Unlike the original, a chunky sauce of carrots, onion, and fennel tops this Americanized version.

1 slightly beaten egg
¼ cup fine dry bread crumbs
3 large cloves garlic, minced
1 teaspoon dried sage, crushed
½ teaspoon salt
¼ teaspoon pepper
1 pound ground veal or lean ground beef
2 tablespoons olive oil
6 dried vermicelli nests (6 ounces total)
2 tablespoons snipped fennel tops
1 tablespoon finely shredded lemon peel
  Lemony Vegetable Sauce
  Snipped fresh parsley and/or fennel tops (optional)

For meatballs, in a large bowl combine egg, bread crumbs, garlic, sage, salt, and pepper. Add ground veal or beef; mix well. Form into 36 meatballs, about 1 inch in size.

In a large skillet heat oil. Add meatballs; cook for 8 to 10 minutes or until brown on all sides and meat is done (160°). Remove meatballs from skillet, reserving drippings for use in Lemony Vegetable Sauce. Cover meatballs; keep warm.

In a large saucepan or Dutch oven cook vermicelli nests according to package directions, stirring the 2 tablespoons fennel tops and the lemon peel into cooking water. Using a slotted spoon, carefully transfer nests to a colander to drain. Cover and keep warm. Prepare Lemony Vegetable Sauce.

To serve, divide the pasta nests among dinner plates. Spoon meatballs into nests. Spoon the sauce over meatballs and pasta nests. If desired, sprinkle with parsley and/or additional fennel tops. Makes 6 servings.

Lemony Vegetable Sauce: Add 2 tablespoons olive oil to the reserved drippings in skillet used for meatballs. Add 1 cup finely chopped onion, 1 cup finely chopped fennel, 1 cup finely chopped carrots, ¼ teaspoon salt, and ¼ teaspoon pepper. Cook and stir over medium heat for 2 minutes. Remove from heat. Stir in ⅓ cup snipped fresh parsley and 1 tablespoon finely shredded lemon peel.

Nutrition information per serving: 352 cal., 16 g total fat (4 g sat. fat), 97 mg chol., 411 mg sodium, 31 g carbo., 21 g pro.

Southwestern Stir-Fry

Just because it comes out of a wok doesn't mean it has to taste Chinese! Made with Mexican ingredients, this stir-fry has a Spanish accent.

1 cup bottled salsa
2 teaspoons cornstarch
8 8-inch flour tortillas
1 tablespoon cooking oil
1 medium green sweet pepper, cut into strips
1 11-ounce can whole kernel corn, drained
3 green onions, bias-sliced into 1-inch pieces (½ cup)
1 pound lean ground beef
10 cherry tomatoes, halved
½ cup shredded cheddar cheese or Monterey Jack cheese with jalapeño peppers (2 ounces)
  Fresh cilantro sprigs (optional)

For sauce, in a small bowl stir together the salsa and cornstarch. Set sauce aside.

Stack tortillas; wrap in foil. Bake in a 350° oven about 10 minutes or until warm. (Or just before serving, microwave tortillas, covered with a paper towel, on 100% power [high] about 1 minute.)

Meanwhile, add cooking oil to a wok or large skillet. Preheat over medium-high heat (add more oil if necessary during cooking). Stir-fry sweet pepper, corn, and green onions in hot oil about 2 minutes or until sweet pepper is crisp-tender. Remove from wok.

Crumble meat into wok. Stir-fry for 2 to 3 minutes or until meat is brown, stirring only as necessary. Drain off fat. Push meat from center.

Stir sauce; add to center of wok. Cook and stir until thickened and bubbly. Return cooked vegetables to wok. Stir all ingredients together to coat. Stir in tomatoes. Cover and cook about 1 minute or until heated through.

Serve immediately with tortillas. Sprinkle with cheese. If desired, garnish with cilantro. Makes 4 servings.

Nutrition information per serving: 634 cal., 29 g total fat (10 g sat. fat), 85 mg chol., 1,042 mg sodium, 64 g carbo., 31 g pro.

Pasta Pizza

This hybrid recipe uses favorite casserole ingredients to create an outstanding dish that looks and tastes like pizza.

5   ounces dried corkscrew pasta (2 cups)
1   beaten egg
¼   cup milk
2   tablespoons grated Parmesan cheese
8   ounces lean ground beef
1   small onion, chopped (⅓ cup)
1   clove garlic, minced
1   14½-ounce can Italian-style stewed
      tomatoes
1   cup green and/or yellow sweet
      pepper cut into 2-inch strips
½   teaspoon dried Italian seasoning,
      crushed
1   4½-ounce jar sliced mushrooms,
      drained
¼   teaspoon crushed red pepper
1   cup shredded mozzarella cheese
      (4 ounces)

Cook pasta according to package directions; drain. Rinse with cold water; drain again.

For pasta crust, in a large bowl combine egg, milk, and Parmesan cheese. Stir in cooked pasta. Spread pasta mixture evenly in a greased 12-inch pizza pan. Bake in a 350° oven for 20 minutes.

Meanwhile, in a large skillet cook meat, onion, and garlic until meat is brown. Drain off fat. Stir in undrained tomatoes (cut up any large pieces), sweet pepper, and Italian seasoning. Bring to boiling; reduce heat. Simmer, uncovered, for 10 to 12 minutes or until sweet pepper is crisp-tender and most of the liquid is evaporated, stirring once or twice. Stir in mushrooms and crushed red pepper.

Spoon the meat mixture over pasta crust. Sprinkle with mozzarella cheese. Bake for 10 to 12 minutes more or until pizza is heated through and cheese is melted. To serve, cut the pizza into wedges. Makes 6 servings.

Nutrition information per serving: 259 cal., 9 g total fat (4 g sat. fat), 72 mg chol., 479 mg sodium, 27 g carbo., 18 g pro.

Ginger-Glazed Pork Chops

For a ready-made glaze, grab a jar of ginger jelly or orange marmalade. The touch of sweetness harmonizes with the ginger-flecked stuffing.

½ cup coarsely chopped fresh mushrooms (such as button, chanterelle, or shiitake)

¼ cup chopped onion

1 tablespoon margarine or butter

1 teaspoon grated fresh ginger

¼ teaspoon salt

¼ teaspoon pepper

1 cup coarsely chopped spinach leaves

¼ cup soft sourdough or white bread crumbs

4 pork loin chops or rib chops, cut 1¼ inches thick (about 3 pounds total)

¼ cup ginger jelly or preserves or orange marmalade

12 green onions

2 teaspoons olive oil

For stuffing, in a medium saucepan cook mushrooms and onion in hot margarine or butter until onion is tender. Remove from heat. Stir in ginger, salt, and pepper. Add chopped spinach and bread crumbs; toss gently to combine.

Trim fat from chops. Make a pocket in each chop by cutting horizontally from the fat side almost to the bone. Spoon stuffing into pockets. Secure openings with wooden toothpicks. Sprinkle chops with additional salt and pepper.

In a covered grill arrange medium-hot coals around a drip pan. Test for medium heat above the pan. Place chops on grill rack over drip pan. Cover and grill for 35 to 40 minutes or until chops are slightly pink in center and juices run clear (160°), turning once and brushing occasionally with ginger jelly or orange marmalade the last 5 minutes of grilling.

Meanwhile, trim roots and tops of green onions. In a medium skillet cook green onions in hot oil for 1 to 3 minutes or until slightly softened. Serve the chops with green onions. Makes 4 servings.

Note: To bake stuffed chops, in a large skillet cook chops on both sides in a small amount of hot oil until brown. Transfer to a baking dish. Cover and bake in a 375° oven for 35 to 45 minutes, brushing occasionally with jelly or marmalade the last 5 minutes of baking.

Nutrition information per serving: 442 cal., 17 g total fat (5 g sat. fat), 132 mg chol., 355 mg sodium, 19 g carbo., 50 g pro.

Spicy Pork Chops

Vegetable juice is the base for this zippy marinade. Add more hot pepper sauce if you like extra heat.

4   boneless pork top loin chops, cut
      ½ inch thick (about 1¼ pounds
      total)
1   6-ounce can (⅔ cup) vegetable juice
2   tablespoons sliced green onion
2   tablespoons canned diced green
      chile peppers
1   teaspoon Worcestershire sauce
1   clove garlic, minced
½   teaspoon dried basil, crushed
      Few dashes bottled hot pepper sauce
2   cups hot cooked orzo or rice

Trim fat from pork chops. Place the chops in a plastic bag set in a shallow bowl.

For marinade, in a small bowl combine the vegetable juice, green onion, green chile peppers, Worcestershire sauce, garlic, basil, and hot pepper sauce. Pour over the chops; seal bag. Marinate in the refrigerator for 2 to 24 hours, turning bag occasionally. Drain chops, reserving marinade.

Place chops on the unheated rack of a broiler pan. Broil 3 to 4 inches from the heat for 5 to 7 minutes or until chops are slightly pink in center and juices run clear (160°), turning once.

In a small saucepan bring the marinade to boiling. Boil gently, uncovered, for 1 minute. Serve the hot marinade with pork chops and hot cooked orzo or rice. Makes 4 servings.

Nutrition information per serving: 273 cal., 11 g total fat (4 g sat. fat), 63 mg chol., 241 mg sodium, 21 g carbo., 22 g pro.

*B*ROILING BASICS

To make sure food is placed correctly for even broiling, use a ruler to measure the distance from the surface of the food to the heating element. If the distance does not match the guidelines in your recipe, adjust the broiler pan or oven rack. *Be sure to measure before turning on the broiler.* To keep cleanup to a minimum, line the broiler pan with foil before sliding the broiler rack into position.

Pork Scaloppine
with Mustard and Rosemary

To keep the pork warm while you prepare the mushroom mixture, place the cooked pork slices on a warm serving platter. Cover with foil and place the platter in a 300° oven.

1 pound pork tenderloin
⅓ cup all-purpose flour
½ teaspoon pepper
¼ teaspoon salt
2 teaspoons margarine or butter
1 tablespoon olive oil or cooking oil
1 cup sliced fresh mushrooms
1 tablespoon snipped fresh rosemary
       or 1 teaspoon dried rosemary,
       crushed
2 cloves garlic, minced
¾ cup chicken broth
2 tablespoons Dijon-style mustard
1 teaspoon finely shredded lemon peel
1 tablespoon lemon juice
   Lemon wedges (optional)
   Fresh rosemary sprigs (optional)

Trim any fat from meat. Cut meat crosswise into ½-inch slices. Place each slice between two pieces of plastic wrap. With the heel of your hand, press each slice until about ⅛ inch thick. Remove plastic wrap.

In a shallow dish combine flour, pepper, and salt. Coat meat with flour mixture, shaking off excess.

In a large skillet heat margarine or butter and oil over medium-high heat. Add half of the meat; cook for 3 to 4 minutes or until slightly pink in center, turning once. Remove from skillet, reserving drippings in skillet. Cover and keep warm. Repeat with the remaining meat.

Reduce heat to medium. Add mushrooms, snipped fresh or dried rosemary, and garlic to reserved drippings in skillet. Cook and stir just until mushrooms are tender. Add broth, scraping up any browned bits on bottom. Bring to boiling. Boil gently, uncovered, about 5 minutes or until reduced by half. Stir in Dijon mustard, lemon peel, and lemon juice. Heat through.

Serve the mushroom mixture over meat. If desired, garnish with lemon wedges and fresh rosemary sprigs. Makes 4 servings.

Nutrition information per serving: 287 cal., 14 g total fat (3 g sat. fat), 81 mg chol., 594 mg sodium, 10 g carbo., 28 g pro.

Pork Tenderloin with Raspberry Sauce

This special-occasion dish features pork tenderloin with a spicy fruit sauce, fresh star fruit, and berries. Choose a seedless jam for the prettiest appearance.

1   pound pork tenderloin
¼   teaspoon black pepper
2   tablespoons margarine or butter
⅓   cup seedless raspberry or strawberry
      jam
2   tablespoons red wine vinegar
2   teaspoons prepared horseradish
1   clove garlic, minced
¼   teaspoon ground red pepper
      Sliced star fruit (optional)
      Raspberries (optional)

Trim any fat from meat. Cut meat crosswise into 1-inch slices. Place each slice between two pieces of plastic wrap. With the heel of your hand, press each slice until about ½ inch thick. Remove plastic wrap. Sprinkle meat with black pepper.

In a 12-inch skillet heat margarine or butter over medium-high heat. Add meat and cook for 4 to 6 minutes or until slightly pink in center, turning once. Remove from skillet, reserving drippings in skillet. Cover and keep warm.

For sauce, stir raspberry or strawberry jam, vinegar, horseradish, garlic, and ground red pepper into reserved drippings in skillet. Cook and stir until bubbly. Cook and stir about 1 minute more or until slightly thickened.

Serve the sauce over meat. If desired, garnish with star fruit and raspberries. Makes 4 servings.

Nutrition information per serving: 282 cal., 10 g total fat (3 g sat. fat), 81 mg chol., 157 mg sodium, 22 g carbo., 25 g pro.

Rhubarb-Glazed Pork Roast

Make this in the spring when rhubarb is in season or buy frozen sliced rhubarb for convenience. You also can make Ginger-Apricot-Glazed Pork Roast (see below).

1 2- to 3-pound boneless pork top
　　loin roast (single loin)
4 cups fresh or frozen sliced rhubarb
½ of a 12-ounce can frozen cranberry-
　　apple juice concentrate
2 tablespoons cornstarch
2 tablespoons cold water
⅓ cup honey
2 tablespoons Dijon-style mustard
1 tablespoon wine vinegar
　　Fresh rosemary sprigs (optional)

Place meat on a rack in a shallow roasting pan. Insert an oven-going meat thermometer into center of meat. Roast in a 325° oven for 1¼ to 1¾ hours or until the thermometer registers 155°.

Meanwhile, for glaze, in a 2-quart saucepan combine rhubarb and cranberry-apple juice concentrate. Bring to boiling; reduce heat. Cover and simmer about 15 minutes or until rhubarb is very tender. Pour mixture through a wire strainer placed over a 2-cup liquid measure, pressing out liquid with the back of a spoon. Add enough water to rhubarb liquid to equal 1¼ cups. Discard pulp.

In the same saucepan stir together cornstarch and cold water. Stir in rhubarb liquid. Cook and stir over medium heat until thickened and bubbly. Cook and stir for 2 minutes more. Stir in honey, mustard, and vinegar. Heat through.

Brush some of the glaze onto the meat the last 30 minutes of roasting. Cover meat with foil; let stand for 15 minutes before slicing. (The meat's temperature will rise 5° during standing.) Heat the remaining glaze; serve with meat. If desired, garnish with rosemary sprigs. Makes 6 to 8 servings.

Nutrition information per serving: 264 cal., 8 g total fat (3 g sat. fat), 51 mg chol., 137 mg sodium, 31 g carbo., 17 g pro.

Ginger-Apricot-Glazed Pork Roast: Prepare as above, except substitute apricot glaze for rhubarb glaze. For apricot glaze, in a small saucepan combine ⅔ cup apricot preserves, 4 teaspoons lime juice, 2 teaspoons soy sauce, ¼ teaspoon grated fresh ginger or ⅛ teaspoon ground ginger, and dash ground red pepper. Cook and stir until mixture is bubbly.

Szechwan Pork with Peppers

Green and red sweet peppers and the spicy sweetness of hoisin sauce contrast nicely with the pleasant heat of this dish. But if you prefer more heat than sweet, simply add more hot bean sauce.

12 ounces lean boneless pork
3 tablespoons bottled hoisin sauce
1 tablespoon hot bean sauce or hot bean paste
1 tablespoon soy sauce
1 teaspoon sugar
1 tablespoon cooking oil
4 cloves garlic, thinly sliced
1 teaspoon grated fresh ginger
2 medium red sweet peppers, cut into 1-inch pieces (2 cups)
2 medium green sweet peppers, cut into 1-inch pieces (2 cups)
2 cups hot cooked noodles or rice

Trim fat from meat. Partially freeze meat. Thinly slice across the grain into bite-size strips. Set aside. For sauce, in a small bowl stir together hoisin sauce, bean sauce or paste, soy sauce, and sugar. Set aside.

Add cooking oil to a wok or large skillet. Preheat over medium-high heat (add more oil if necessary during cooking). Stir-fry garlic and ginger in hot oil for 15 seconds. Add sweet peppers; stir-fry for 3 to 4 minutes or until crisp-tender. Remove pepper mixture from wok.

Add meat to wok. Stir-fry for 2 to 3 minutes or until meat is slightly pink in center. Push meat from center of wok. Add sauce to center of wok. Cook and stir until bubbly.

Return pepper mixture to wok. Stir all ingredients together to coat. Cook and stir about 1 minute more or until heated through. Serve immediately over hot cooked noodles or rice. Makes 4 servings.

Nutrition information per serving: 292 cal., 10 g total fat (3 g sat. fat), 63 mg chol., 1,324 mg sodium, 32 g carbo., 18 g pro.

GREAT-TASTING GINGER

Many stir-fries depend on spicy-sweet ginger for its tempting flavor. Look for this knobby root in your supermarket's produce section. Grate or slice as much as you need (peeling isn't necessary). Wrap the remaining root in paper towels and refrigerate it up to 1 week. Or cut up the ginger and place it in a small jar. Fill the jar with dry sherry or wine and refrigerate it, covered, up to 3 months.

Jamaican Pork and Sweet Potato Stir-Fry

Take a vacation from the postwork, predinner rush with this Jamaica-inspired dish, which features two of the easygoing island's favorite ingredients: lean pork and golden sweet potatoes. For flavor, pick up Jamaican jerk seasoning at the grocery store or make your own seasoning.

1½ cups instant white rice
2 green onions, thinly sliced (¼ cup)
1 large sweet potato (about 12 ounces)
1 medium tart apple (such as Granny Smith), cored
12 ounces lean boneless pork strips for stir-frying
2 to 3 teaspoons purchased Jamaican jerk seasoning or Homemade Jamaican Jerk Seasoning
1 tablespoon cooking oil
⅓ cup apple juice or water

Prepare rice according to package directions. Stir half of the green onions into cooked rice.

Meanwhile, peel sweet potato. Cut into quarters lengthwise, then thinly slice crosswise. Place in a microwave-safe pie plate or shallow dish. Cover with vented plastic wrap. Microwave on 100% power (high) for 3 to 4 minutes or until tender, stirring once. Cut apple into 16 wedges. Sprinkle meat strips with jerk seasoning; toss to coat.

Add cooking oil to a wok or large skillet. Preheat over medium-high heat (add more oil if necessary during cooking). Stir-fry meat in hot oil for 2 minutes. Add apple and remaining green onions. Stir-fry for 1 to 2 minutes more or until meat is slightly pink in center.

Stir in sweet potato and apple juice or water. Bring to boiling; reduce heat. Simmer, uncovered, for 1 minute. Serve immediately over hot cooked rice mixture. Makes 4 servings.

Homemade Jamaican Jerk Seasoning: In a small bowl combine 1 teaspoon crushed red pepper; ½ teaspoon ground allspice; ¼ teaspoon curry powder; ¼ teaspoon coarsely ground black pepper; ⅛ teaspoon dried thyme, crushed; ⅛ teaspoon ground red pepper; and ⅛ teaspoon ground ginger.

Nutrition information per serving: 365 cal., 9 g total fat (2 g sat. fat), 38 mg chol., 131 mg sodium, 54 g carbo., 16 g pro.

Country-Style Oven Ribs

The secret ingredient in the sweet dark basting sauce keeps your family guessing—it's root beer! For a complete meal, serve the ribs with a side dish of crisp, refreshing vegetables or coleslaw.

1½	teaspoons salt
1	teaspoon ground cumin
1	teaspoon paprika
½	teaspoon pepper
½	teaspoon ground cinnamon
¼	teaspoon ground cloves
3½	pounds pork country-style ribs
4	cups root beer (not low calorie)
⅓	cup bottled barbecue sauce
2	tablespoons tomato paste
1	tablespoon vinegar
2	teaspoons Dijon-style mustard
1	teaspoon Worcestershire sauce

In a small bowl combine the salt, cumin, paprika, pepper, cinnamon, and cloves. Sprinkle ribs with spice mixture, rubbing it over entire surface. Place ribs, bone sides up, in a shallow roasting pan. Cover and bake in a 350° oven for 1¼ hours.

Meanwhile, for sauce, in a large saucepan bring root beer to boiling. Boil gently, uncovered, for 20 to 25 minutes or until root beer is reduced to 1¼ cups. Remove from heat. Stir in the barbecue sauce, tomato paste, vinegar, mustard, and Worcestershire sauce. Return to boiling. Boil gently, uncovered, for 1 minute. Remove from heat.

Drain fat from ribs. Turn ribs meaty sides up. Spoon about half of the sauce over ribs. Bake for 45 minutes more, basting once or twice with more of the sauce. To serve, spoon the remaining sauce over ribs. Makes 4 servings.

Nutrition information per serving: 549 cal., 24 g total fat (8 g sat. fat), 99 mg chol., 1,186 mg sodium, 32 g carbo., 49 g pro.

Provolone and Ham Melt

This sandwich satisfies both children and adults. Variations include cheese, ham, and fruit, or red sweet pepper and prosciutto.

8 slices thick-cut multigrain, whole wheat, poppy seed, white, or pumpernickel bread
   Margarine or butter, softened
4 teaspoons mayonnaise or salad dressing
4 ounces provolone and/or cheddar cheese, thinly sliced
½ of a 7-ounce jar roasted red sweet peppers, well drained
½ of a small pear or apple, thinly sliced, or 2 canned pineapple rings, well drained and patted dry
4 ounces thinly sliced cooked ham or prosciutto
2 tablespoons mango chutney
   Fresh fruit (such as sliced pears or apples, pineapple wedges, and/or grapes) (optional)

Spread one side of each bread slice with margarine or butter. Place 4 bread slices, buttered sides down, on a griddle. Spread mayonnaise or salad dressing on the slices on griddle. Top with provolone and/or cheddar cheese. Top 2 of the bread slices with roasted red peppers and the other 2 slices with sliced pear or apple or pineapple rings. Top all bread slices on griddle with ham or prosciutto.

Cut up large pieces of chutney; spread the unbuttered sides of the remaining 4 bread slices with chutney. Place, buttered sides up, on top of bread slices on griddle.

Cook sandwiches over medium heat about 8 minutes or until bread is toasted and cheese is melted, turning once. If desired, serve with additional fruit. Makes 4 servings.

Nutrition information per serving: 398 cal., 22 g total fat (10 g sat. fat), 53 mg chol., 970 mg sodium, 35 g carbo., 17 g pro.

Cheesy Ham and Linguine

Make this meal even easier by buying cut-up vegetables from your grocery store's salad bar.

6 ounces dried spinach and/or plain
   linguine
2 medium carrots, cut into ½-inch
   pieces (1 cup)
1 cup broccoli florets
1 cup sliced fresh mushrooms
2 tablespoons margarine or butter
2 tablespoons all-purpose flour
1 tablespoon snipped fresh parsley
½ teaspoon dried basil, crushed
1¼ cups milk
6 ounces sliced cooked ham, cut
   into bite-size strips
½ cup shredded cheddar cheese
   (2 ounces)

In a Dutch oven or large saucepan cook pasta and carrots in a large amount of boiling salted water for 7 minutes, stirring occasionally. Add broccoli florets. Return to boiling and cook for 3 to 5 minutes more or until pasta is tender but slightly firm and vegetables are crisp-tender; drain. Cover and keep warm.

Meanwhile, in a medium saucepan cook mushrooms in hot margarine or butter until tender. Stir in flour, parsley, and basil. Add milk all at once. Cook and stir until thickened and bubbly. Add ham and cheddar cheese, stirring until cheese is melted. Pour cheese mixture over pasta and vegetables; toss gently to coat. Makes 4 servings.

Nutrition information per serving: 417 cal., 15 g total fat (6 g sat. fat), 33 mg chol., 711 mg sodium, 47 g carbo., 23 g pro.

Sausage, Broccoli, and Pasta Toss

No time to cook? Here's a quick-and-easy dish to serve in a pinch.

1 cup dried tricolor or plain tortellini
   (about ½ of a 7-ounce package)
3 cups broccoli florets
8 ounces cooked smoked Polish
   sausage, halved lengthwise and
   thinly bias-sliced
1 tablespoon margarine or butter
1 tablespoon all-purpose flour
1 teaspoon caraway seeds
1 cup milk
1 cup shredded process Swiss cheese
   (4 ounces)
1 tablespoon coarse-grain brown
   mustard

In a Dutch oven or large saucepan cook tortellini in a large amount of boiling salted water for 10 minutes, stirring occasionally. Add broccoli and sausage. Return to boiling and cook about 5 minutes more or until pasta is tender but slightly firm and broccoli is crisp-tender; drain. Cover and keep warm.

Meanwhile, in a medium saucepan melt margarine or butter. Stir in flour and caraway seeds. Add milk all at once. Cook and stir until thickened and bubbly. Add Swiss cheese and mustard, stirring until cheese is melted. Pour over the tortellini mixture; toss gently to coat. Makes 4 servings.

Nutrition information per serving: 482 cal., 31 g total fat (12 g sat. fat), 70 mg chol., 925 mg sodium, 25 g carbo., 26 g pro.

Sausage and Bean Rigatoni

Reminiscent of a wonderful baked Italian casserole that comes bubbling from the oven, this dish cooks on the stovetop instead, so it's ready for the table in less than half the time.

8   ounces dried rigatoni pasta
1   15-ounce can white kidney (cannellini), Great Northern, or navy beans, rinsed and drained
1   14½-ounce can Italian-style stewed tomatoes
6   ounces light cooked smoked sausage or turkey sausage, sliced ½ inch thick
⅓   cup finely shredded or snipped fresh basil
¼   cup shaved or finely shredded Asiago cheese (1 ounce)

Cook pasta according to package directions, except omit any salt; drain. Cover and keep warm.

Meanwhile, in a large saucepan combine beans, undrained tomatoes, and sausage; heat through. Add bean mixture and basil to cooked pasta; toss gently to mix. Sprinkle each serving with Asiago cheese. Makes 4 servings.

Nutrition information per serving: 401 cal., 6 g total fat (1 g sat. fat), 32 mg chol., 964 mg sodium, 67 g carbo., 25 g pro.

*B*EYOND RED KIDNEY BEANS

When you think of kidney beans, the red ones probably come to mind. But their Italian cousins, the white cannellini beans, also are a versatile and delicious choice. These mild-tasting legumes are ideal for making casseroles, soups, stews, and other one-dish meals, such as Sausage and Bean Rigatoni (above). Cannellini come in both canned and dried forms. Look for them where you find the other canned or dried beans in your supermarket or at Italian food specialty stores.

Poultry

Contents

For more recipes, visit our Recipe Center at www.bhg.com/bkrecipe

Chicken Breasts with Burgundy Sauce

The combination of orange marmalade and Burgundy lends a wonderfully fruity flavor to these grilled chicken breasts.

¼ cup orange marmalade
½ teaspoon cornstarch
¼ teaspoon salt
¼ cup Burgundy wine
4 medium skinless, boneless chicken breast halves (about 1 pound total)
Hot cooked pasta (optional)
Fresh thyme sprigs (optional)
Orange slices, halved (optional)

For sauce, in a small saucepan combine orange marmalade, cornstarch, and salt. Stir in Burgundy. Cook and stir over medium heat until thickened and bubbly. Cook and stir for 2 minutes more. Set sauce aside.

Place chicken on the rack of an uncovered grill directly over medium coals. Grill for 12 to 15 minutes or until chicken is no longer pink (170°), turning and brushing once with sauce.

(Or in a covered grill arrange medium-hot coals around a drip pan. Test for medium heat above the pan. Place chicken on grill rack over drip pan. Cover and grill for 15 to 18 minutes. Brush occasionally with sauce during the last 10 minutes of grilling.)

Before serving, brush chicken with any remaining sauce. If desired, serve chicken over hot cooked pasta and garnish with fresh thyme and orange slices. Makes 4 servings.

Nutrition information per serving: 184 cal., 3 g total fat (1 g sat. fat), 59 mg chol., 199 mg sodium, 15 g carbo., 22 g pro.

Pollo Relleno

Expect oohs and aahs when you serve these chicken rolls; each has a cheese-stuffed chile pepper inside.

6   medium skinless, boneless chicken
    breast halves (about 1½ pounds
    total)
⅓   cup yellow cornmeal
½   of a 1¼-ounce package (2 tablespoons)
    taco seasoning mix
1   egg
1   4-ounce can whole green chile
    peppers, rinsed, seeded, and cut
    in half lengthwise (6 pieces total)
2   ounces Monterey Jack cheese, cut
    into six 2×½-inch sticks
2   tablespoons snipped fresh cilantro
    or parsley
¼   teaspoon black pepper
¼   teaspoon crushed red pepper
1   8-ounce jar taco sauce or salsa
½   cup shredded Monterey Jack or
    cheddar cheese (optional)
    Fresh cilantro sprigs (optional)

Place each chicken piece between two pieces of plastic wrap. Pound lightly with the flat side of a meat mallet until about ⅛ inch thick. Remove plastic wrap.

In a shallow bowl combine cornmeal and taco seasoning mix. Place egg in another shallow bowl; beat lightly.

For each chicken roll, place a chile pepper half on a chicken piece near an edge. Place a cheese stick on top of chile pepper. Sprinkle with some of the snipped cilantro or parsley, black pepper, and red pepper. Fold in sides; starting from edge with cheese, roll up chicken.

Dip chicken rolls into egg and roll in cornmeal mixture to coat. Place rolls, seam sides down, in a shallow baking pan. Bake in a 375° oven for 25 to 30 minutes or until chicken is no longer pink.

Heat taco sauce or salsa. If desired, sprinkle chicken rolls with shredded cheese. Serve with taco sauce or salsa. If desired, garnish with cilantro sprigs. Makes 6 servings.

Nutrition information per serving: 235 cal., 10 g total fat (3 g sat. fat), 103 mg chol., 769 mg sodium, 13 g carbo., 28 g pro.

Chicken with Golden Raisins and Pine Nuts

Italians frequently use pine nuts, also called pignoli, in pasta sauces, pesto, rice dishes, and cookies. Refrigerate pine nuts in an airtight container up to two months or freeze them up to six months to prevent them from turning rancid.

1	medium onion, cut into thin slivers
2	cloves garlic, minced
1	tablespoon olive oil
1½	pounds meaty chicken pieces (breast halves, thighs, and drumsticks), skinned
½	cup white wine vinegar
¼	teaspoon salt
⅛	teaspoon pepper
1	cup reduced-sodium chicken broth
½	cup golden raisins
2	teaspoons snipped fresh thyme or ½ teaspoon dried thyme, crushed
1	teaspoon snipped fresh rosemary or ¼ teaspoon dried rosemary, crushed
1	tablespoon cold water
1½	teaspoons cornstarch
2	tablespoons pine nuts, toasted

In a large nonstick skillet cook onion and garlic in hot oil over medium heat for 1 minute. Add chicken pieces and cook for 10 to 15 minutes or until brown, turning to brown evenly. Drain well.

Add the vinegar, salt, and pepper to chicken in skillet. Bring to boiling. Cook, uncovered, over high heat about 5 minutes or until vinegar is nearly evaporated, turning chicken once. Carefully add broth, raisins, thyme, and rosemary. Bring to boiling; reduce heat. Cover and simmer for 30 to 35 minutes or until chicken is no longer pink (170° for breasts; 180° for thighs and drumsticks).

To serve, transfer chicken to a serving platter. For sauce, combine cold water and cornstarch; stir into broth mixture in skillet. Cook and stir until thickened and bubbly. Cook and stir for 2 minutes more. Spoon some of the sauce over chicken; pass the remaining sauce. Sprinkle the chicken with pine nuts. Makes 4 servings.

Nutrition information per serving: 269 cal., 10 g total fat (2 g sat. fat), 71 mg chol., 334 mg sodium, 22 g carbo., 24 g pro.

Quick Chicken Mole

Declare a Mexican theme night by serving this dish with warm flour tortillas, tomato salsa seasoned with snipped fresh cilantro, and sliced oranges layered with coconut for dessert.

6   medium chicken breast halves
      (about 3 pounds total)
2   tablespoons olive oil or cooking oil
1   small onion, chopped
1½ teaspoons chili powder
1   teaspoon sesame seeds
1   clove garlic, minced
¼   teaspoon salt
¼   teaspoon ground cumin
¼   teaspoon ground cinnamon
1   small tomato, chopped
1   tomatillo, peeled and cut into wedges,
      or 1 small tomato, chopped
½   cup chicken broth
½   cup tomato sauce
2   tablespoons raisins
2   teaspoons unsweetened cocoa
      powder
    Several dashes bottled hot pepper
      sauce
    Hot cooked rice
    Pumpkin seeds or slivered almonds,
      toasted (optional)

Skin chicken. In a large skillet cook chicken in hot oil over medium heat about 10 minutes or until light brown, turning to brown evenly. Add onion, chili powder, sesame seeds, garlic, salt, cumin, and cinnamon. Cook and stir for 30 seconds.

Stir in tomato, tomatillo, chicken broth, tomato sauce, raisins, cocoa powder, and hot pepper sauce. Bring to boiling; reduce heat. Simmer, uncovered, about 15 minutes or until chicken is no longer pink (170°). Using a slotted spoon, remove chicken pieces from skillet. Simmer the tomato mixture, uncovered, for 4 to 5 minutes or to desired consistency.

To serve, spoon tomato mixture over chicken and rice. If desired, sprinkle with pumpkin seeds or almonds. Makes 6 servings.

Nutrition information per serving: 367 cal., 9 g total fat (2 g sat. fat), 76 mg chol., 543 mg sodium, 37 g carbo., 33 g pro.

GARLIC HINTS

Working with garlic is easy if you know how to handle it. Loosen the garlic skin quickly by crushing each clove with the flat side of a chef's knife. The skin will slip off. To mince the peeled garlic, place it in a garlic press or use a sharp knife to cut it into tiny pieces. If you prefer, use bottled minced garlic (usually found in your supermarket's produce section) instead of the cloves.

Chicken with Peach Salsa

If fresh peaches or papayas aren't in season, thaw and chop 1 cup frozen unsweetened peach slices.

2 tablespoons lime juice
4 teaspoons teriyaki sauce or soy sauce
4 medium skinless, boneless chicken breast halves (about 1 pound total)
1 medium peach, peeled, pitted, and chopped, or ½ of a medium papaya, peeled, seeded, and chopped (about 1 cup)
1 small tomato, chopped (½ cup)
2 tablespoons sliced green onion
1 tablespoon lime juice
1 teaspoon grated fresh ginger or ¼ teaspoon ground ginger
¼ teaspoon bottled minced garlic or ⅛ teaspoon garlic powder
Hot cooked rice (optional)
Fresh thyme sprigs (optional)

For marinade, in a small bowl stir together the 2 tablespoons lime juice and the teriyaki sauce or soy sauce. Brush both sides of chicken with marinade. Cover and marinate at room temperature for 30 minutes or in the refrigerator up to 2 hours.

For salsa, in a medium bowl stir together peach or papaya, tomato, green onion, the 1 tablespoon lime juice, the ginger, and garlic or garlic powder. Cover and let stand at room temperature for 30 minutes or chill up to 2 hours.

Place the chicken on the unheated rack of a broiler pan. Broil 4 to 5 inches from the heat for 12 to 15 minutes or until no longer pink (170°), turning once.

If desired, serve chicken and salsa over hot cooked rice and garnish with thyme. Makes 4 servings.

Nutrition information per serving: 146 cal., 3 g total fat (1 g sat. fat), 59 mg chol., 287 mg sodium, 6 g carbo., 22 g pro.

Chicken and Mushrooms

Whether to slice the mushrooms or not depends on their size. If they're larger than 1½ inches in diameter, slice them. Otherwise leave them whole.

4	chicken thighs
4	chicken drumsticks
¼	cup all-purpose flour
¼	teaspoon salt
¼	teaspoon pepper
¼	teaspoon paprika
2	tablespoons cooking oil
2	cups whole or sliced fresh mushrooms
1	medium red sweet pepper, cut into 1-inch strips
1	medium onion, sliced
3	cloves garlic, minced
½	cup dry red wine or beef broth
2	tablespoons balsamic vinegar
1	14½-ounce can diced tomatoes
2	teaspoons dried Italian seasoning, crushed
¼	cup half-and-half or light cream
1	tablespoon all-purpose flour
	Hot cooked pasta (optional)
¼	cup snipped fresh Italian flat-leaf parsley

Skin chicken. In a large self-sealing plastic bag combine the ¼ cup flour, the salt, pepper, and paprika. Add 2 or 3 pieces of chicken to the bag at a time. Seal and shake to coat well.

In a very large skillet heat the 2 tablespoons oil over medium heat. Cook the chicken in hot oil for 10 to 15 minutes or until brown, turning to brown evenly. Remove chicken from skillet, reserving drippings in skillet.

Add mushrooms, sweet pepper, onion, and garlic to the reserved drippings in skillet. Cook and stir for 2 minutes. Add red wine or beef broth and balsamic vinegar. Cook and stir for 5 minutes more. Stir in undrained tomatoes and Italian seasoning.

Bring to boiling, scraping up any browned bits on bottom of skillet. Return chicken to skillet; reduce heat. Cover and simmer about 20 minutes or until chicken is no longer pink (180°). Remove chicken; cover and keep warm.

Stir together half-and-half or light cream and the 1 tablespoon flour; stir into tomato mixture. Cook and stir until slightly thickened and bubbly. Cook and stir for 1 minute more. Return chicken to skillet; heat through. If desired, serve over hot cooked pasta. Sprinkle with parsley. Makes 4 to 6 servings.

Nutrition information per serving: 323 cal., 13 g total fat (3 g sat. fat), 89 mg chol., 400 mg sodium, 21 g carbo., 25 g pro.

Chicken and Prosciutto Roll-Ups

This pretty dish takes the Italian technique braciola—wrapping thin slices of meat around savories such as Italian ham, cheese, artichokes, spinach, and herbs—and applies it to chicken. Serve these attractive spirals with spinach fettuccine.

¼ cup dry white wine
2 teaspoons snipped fresh thyme or
    ½ teaspoon dried thyme, crushed
4 medium skinless, boneless chicken
    breast halves (about 1 pound
    total)
4 thin slices prosciutto (about
    1 ounce total), trimmed of fat
2 ounces fontina cheese, thinly sliced
½ of a 7-ounce jar roasted red sweet
    peppers, cut into thin strips
    (about ½ cup)
    Fresh thyme sprigs (optional)

For sauce, in a small bowl combine wine and the snipped fresh or dried thyme. Set aside.

Place each chicken piece between two pieces of plastic wrap. Pound lightly with the flat side of a meat mallet until about ⅛ inch thick. Remove plastic wrap.

For each chicken roll, place a slice of prosciutto and one-fourth of the cheese on a chicken piece near an edge. Arrange one-fourth of the roasted pepper strips on top of cheese. Fold in the sides; starting from edge with pepper strips, roll up chicken. Secure with wooden toothpicks. (If desired, wrap each chicken roll in plastic wrap and chill up to 4 hours.)

Place chicken rolls on the rack of an uncovered grill directly over medium coals. Grill for 15 to 17 minutes or until chicken is no longer pink, turning to cook evenly and brushing twice with sauce. Remove the toothpicks. If desired, garnish chicken rolls with fresh thyme sprigs. Makes 4 servings.

Nutrition information per serving: 214 cal., 9 g total fat (4 g sat. fat), 76 mg chol., 294 mg sodium, 2 g carbo., 27 g pro.

Fruit-Stuffed Roasted Chicken

While the bird roasts to perfection, tuck some rice pudding in the oven to bake alongside.

1	4½- to 5-pound whole roasting chicken
¼	cup margarine or butter, melted
¼	cup dry sherry
4½	teaspoons snipped fresh thyme or 1½ teaspoons dried thyme, crushed
2	teaspoons finely shredded orange peel
2	medium apples, cored and chopped (2 cups)
1	medium onion, chopped (½ cup)
½	cup chopped celery
2	cups French bread cut into ¾-inch cubes
10	pitted dried plums (prunes) or dried apricots, cut up
1	cup seedless green grapes, halved
2	tablespoons orange juice

Rinse chicken; pat dry with paper towels. Sprinkle body cavity with salt and pepper. In a small bowl combine 2 tablespoons of the melted margarine or butter, 2 tablespoons of the sherry, 1 tablespoon of the fresh thyme or 1 teaspoon of the dried thyme, and 1 teaspoon of the orange peel. Brush chicken with sherry mixture.

For stuffing, in a medium skillet cook apples, onion, and celery in the remaining melted margarine or butter about 5 minutes or until tender. In a large bowl combine apple mixture, French bread, dried plums or apricots, grapes, orange juice, remaining sherry, remaining fresh or dried thyme, and remaining orange peel. (Stuffing will become more moist while cooking.)

Spoon some of the stuffing loosely into neck cavity of chicken. Pull neck skin to back; fasten with a small skewer. Lightly spoon the remaining stuffing into body cavity. Tuck drumsticks under band of skin that crosses tail. If there is no band, tie drumsticks to tail. Twist wing tips under chicken. Place chicken, breast side up, on a rack in a shallow roasting pan. Insert an oven-going meat thermometer into center of an inside thigh muscle, not touching bone.

Roast in a 375° oven for 1¼ hours. Cut band of skin or string between drumsticks so thighs will cook evenly. Roast for 30 minutes to 1 hour more or until drumsticks move easily in their sockets and thermometer registers 180°. (Center of stuffing should reach 165°.)

Remove from oven. Cover the chicken with foil; let stand for 10 to 15 minutes before carving. Makes 10 servings.

Nutrition information per serving: 393 cal., 18 g total fat (5 g sat. fat), 93 mg chol., 250 mg sodium, 22 g carbo., 33 g pro.

Skewered Chicken with Papaya Chutney

To round out this meal, accompany chicken kabobs with steamed rice spiked with dried crushed red pepper.

Papaya Chutney
1 medium onion, cut into 8 wedges
1 tablespoon curry powder
2 tablespoons olive oil or cooking oil
2 tablespoons lemon juice
1 tablespoon water
½ teaspoon salt
¼ teaspoon pepper
1 pound skinless, boneless chicken breast halves or thighs
1 red or green sweet pepper, cut into 1-inch pieces
12 fresh or canned pineapple chunks

Prepare Papaya Chutney. In a small saucepan cook onion in a small amount of boiling water for 4 minutes; drain. Set aside.

Meanwhile, in a small skillet cook and stir curry powder in hot oil for 30 seconds. Remove from heat. Stir in lemon juice, water, salt, and pepper. Set aside.

Cut chicken into 1-inch pieces. Alternately thread chicken, red or green sweet pepper, pineapple, and onion onto 4 long metal skewers. Stir curry mixture; brush over kabobs.

Place kabobs on the rack of an uncovered grill directly over medium coals. Grill for 12 to 14 minutes or until chicken is no longer pink, turning occasionally to brown evenly. (Or place on the unheated rack of a broiler pan. Broil 4 to 5 inches from the heat for 10 to 12 minutes, turning occasionally to brown evenly.) Serve the kabobs with chutney. Makes 4 servings.

Papaya Chutney: In a medium saucepan combine 1 cup chopped, peeled apple; 1 cup chopped, peeled papaya; ¼ cup packed brown sugar; 2 tablespoons raisins; 2 tablespoons chopped green sweet pepper; 2 tablespoons vinegar; 2 tablespoons water; 2 teaspoons lemon juice; and dash salt. Bring to boiling; reduce heat. Simmer, uncovered, about 15 minutes or until fruit is tender and chutney is desired consistency, stirring occasionally.

Nutrition information per serving: 337 cal., 11 g total fat (2 g sat. fat), 59 mg chol., 384 mg sodium, 40 g carbo., 23 g pro.

Chicken Fajitas with Guacamole

Make this chunky guacamole up to four hours before serving. Just keep it covered and refrigerated so it won't darken.

12 ounces skinless, boneless chicken
    breast halves
¼   cup snipped fresh cilantro or parsley
¼   cup olive oil or cooking oil
1   teaspoon finely shredded lemon peel
2   tablespoons lemon juice
1   teaspoon chili powder
½   teaspoon ground cumin
½   teaspoon pepper
8   8-inch flour tortillas
2   cups shredded lettuce
1   cup shredded cheddar cheese
    (4 ounces)
1   large tomato, chopped
½   cup sliced pitted ripe olives
    Guacamole

Place chicken in a plastic bag set in a shallow dish. For marinade, in a small bowl combine cilantro or parsley, oil, lemon peel, lemon juice, chili powder, cumin, and pepper. Pour over chicken; seal bag. Marinate in the refrigerator for 1 hour, turning bag occasionally. Drain chicken, reserving marinade.

Place chicken on the rack of an uncovered grill directly over medium coals. Grill for 12 to 15 minutes or until chicken is no longer pink (170°), turning and brushing once with reserved marinade. (Or place on the unheated rack of a broiler pan. Broil 4 to 5 inches from the heat for 12 to 15 minutes, turning and brushing once with reserved marinade.) Stack tortillas; wrap in foil. Heat on grill or in oven the last 5 minutes of cooking.

Cut chicken into bite-size strips. To assemble fajitas, arrange chicken strips, lettuce, cheese, tomato, and olives on warm tortillas. Fold or roll up tortillas. Serve with Guacamole. Makes 4 servings.

Guacamole: Seed and peel 1 ripe avocado. In a small bowl coarsely mash avocado. Stir in 1 medium tomato, seeded, chopped, and drained; 2 tablespoons finely chopped onion; 1 tablespoon lemon juice; and ¼ teaspoon salt. Cover the surface with plastic wrap and chill up to 4 hours.

Nutrition information per serving: 576 cal., 32 g total fat (10 g sat. fat), 74 mg chol., 745 mg sodium, 45 g carbo., 30 g pro.

Chicken Fingers with Honey Sauce

Serve your favorite barbecue sauce as a quick alternative to the honey sauce.

12	ounces skinless, boneless chicken breast halves
2	slightly beaten egg whites
1	tablespoon honey
2	cups cornflakes, crushed
¼	teaspoon pepper
¼	cup honey
4	teaspoons prepared mustard or Dijon-style mustard
¼	teaspoon garlic powder

Cut chicken into 3×¾-inch strips. In a small bowl combine egg whites and the 1 tablespoon honey. In a shallow dish combine crushed cornflakes and pepper. Dip chicken strips in egg white mixture and roll in cornflake mixture to coat.

Place chicken in a single layer on an ungreased baking sheet. Bake in a 450° oven for 11 to 13 minutes or until chicken is no longer pink.

Meanwhile, for sauce, in a small bowl stir together the ¼ cup honey, the mustard, and garlic powder. Serve the chicken strips with sauce. Makes 4 servings.

Nutrition information per serving: 230 cal., 2 g total fat (1 g sat. fat), 45 mg chol., 275 mg sodium, 31 g carbo., 19 g pro.

Fruity Chicken Salad Sandwiches

For a special touch, pick up a hearty wheat bread from your favorite bakery.

2	cups chopped cooked chicken breast (10 ounces)
1	small Red Delicious or Granny Smith apple, cored and chopped
⅓	cup sliced celery
¼	cup raisins
1	green onion, thinly sliced
¼	cup plain fat-free yogurt
¼	cup bottled reduced-calorie ranch salad dressing
	Red-tipped leaf lettuce
8	slices whole wheat or other bread

In a large bowl stir together the chicken, apple, celery, raisins, and green onion. In a small bowl combine yogurt and ranch salad dressing. Pour over chicken mixture; toss gently to coat.

Arrange lettuce leaves on half of the bread slices. Spread chicken mixture on lettuce. Top with the remaining bread. Makes 4 servings.

Nutrition information per serving: 332 cal., 8 g total fat (1 g sat. fat), 65 mg chol., 590 mg sodium, 38 g carbo., 29 g pro.

Chicken Fingers with Honey Sauce

Swiss Chicken Bundles

This tarragon-laced lasagna makes an elegant dish for a bridal or baby shower.

8 dried lasagna noodles
1 beaten egg
2 cups ricotta cheese or cream-style cottage cheese, drained
1½ cups chopped cooked chicken or turkey
1½ teaspoons snipped fresh tarragon or basil or ¼ teaspoon dried tarragon or basil, crushed
2 tablespoons margarine or butter
2 tablespoons all-purpose flour
½ teaspoon dry mustard
¼ teaspoon salt
⅛ teaspoon pepper
1½ cups milk
1½ cups shredded process Swiss cheese (6 ounces)
Paprika or snipped fresh parsley (optional)
Fresh tarragon sprigs (optional)

Cook lasagna noodles according to package directions; drain. Rinse with cold water; drain again.

Meanwhile, for filling, in a medium bowl stir together egg, ricotta or cottage cheese, chicken or turkey, and the snipped fresh or dried tarragon or basil.

Grease a 2-quart rectangular baking dish; set aside. To assemble bundles, spread about ⅓ cup of the filling over each lasagna noodle. Starting from a short end, roll up lasagna noodles. Place the bundles, seam sides down, in the prepared baking dish; set aside.

For sauce, in a medium saucepan melt margarine or butter. Stir in flour, mustard, salt, and pepper. Add milk all at once. Cook and stir until thickened and bubbly. Gradually add cheese, stirring until melted after each addition. Pour sauce over lasagna bundles.

Cover and bake in a 375° oven for 30 to 35 minutes or until heated through. Let stand for 10 minutes. Transfer lasagna bundles to dinner plates. Stir sauce in baking dish; spoon the sauce over bundles. If desired, sprinkle with paprika or parsley and garnish with fresh tarragon sprigs. Makes 8 servings.

Nutrition information per serving: 347 cal., 17 g total fat (8 g sat. fat), 92 mg chol., 523 mg sodium, 22 g carbo., 25 g pro.

Saucy Chicken Rigatoni

While cooking this single-saucepan dinner, stir every now and then to prevent the pasta from sticking to the pan.

1 medium onion, chopped (½ cup)
1 clove garlic, minced
1 tablespoon cooking oil
1 14½-ounce can tomatoes, cut up
1 7½-ounce can tomatoes, cut up
2 cups dried rigatoni pasta or elbow macaroni
1¼ cups water
1 2½-ounce jar sliced mushrooms, drained
1 teaspoon dried Italian seasoning, crushed
⅛ teaspoon ground red pepper (optional)
1½ cups chopped cooked chicken or turkey
   Fresh basil leaves (optional)

In a large saucepan cook onion and garlic in hot oil until tender. Stir in both cans of undrained tomatoes, the pasta, water, mushrooms, Italian seasoning, and, if desired, ground red pepper.

Bring to boiling; reduce heat. Cover and simmer about 20 minutes or until pasta is tender but still firm, stirring occasionally.

Stir chicken or turkey into pasta mixture; heat through. If desired, garnish with basil. Makes 4 servings.

Nutrition information per serving: 293 cal., 9 g total fat (2 g sat. fat), 51 mg chol., 399 mg sodium, 32 g carbo., 22 g pro.

Chicken, Bean, and Tomato Stir-Fry

If you think good taste is hard to measure, consider cooking with Chinese long beans. A star of Asian stir-fries, these dark green, pencil-thin legumes average 1½ feet of crunchy flavor.

6   ounces dried wide rice noodles or egg noodles
12 ounces skinless, boneless chicken breast halves
1   teaspoon Cajun seasoning or other spicy seasoning blend
4   teaspoons cooking oil
2   cloves garlic, minced
1   pound whole Chinese long beans or green beans, cut into 3-inch pieces
¼   cup water
2   medium tomatoes, cut into thin wedges
2   tablespoons raspberry vinegar

Cook rice noodles in boiling, lightly salted water for 3 to 5 minutes or until tender. (Or cook egg noodles according to package directions.) Drain; cover and keep warm. Meanwhile, cut chicken into thin bite-size strips. Combine chicken and Cajun or other seasoning blend; toss to coat. Set aside.

Add 2 teaspoons of the oil to a large skillet. Preheat over medium-high heat. Stir-fry garlic in hot oil for 15 seconds. Add beans. Stir-fry for 2 minutes. Add water; reduce heat to low. Cover and simmer for 6 to 8 minutes or until beans are crisp-tender. Remove from skillet.

Add the remaining oil to skillet. Add chicken. Stir-fry for 2 to 3 minutes or until no longer pink. Return cooked beans to skillet. Add tomatoes and vinegar. Stir all ingredients together to coat. Cook and stir for 1 to 2 minutes more or until heated through. Serve immediately over hot cooked noodles. Makes 4 servings.

Nutrition information per serving: 361 cal., 5 g total fat (1 g sat. fat), 45 mg chol., 334 mg sodium, 54 g carbo., 25 g pro.

STIR-FRYING GARLIC

To evenly distribute garlic flavor to stir-fry ingredients, season the oil first. Add the garlic to the hot oil, moving it constantly so it doesn't burn. After about 15 seconds, begin adding the other stir-fry ingredients to the oil.

Broccoli Chicken Stir-Fry

Shredded lettuce instead of the usual rice adds a pleasant crispness and lightness to this stir-fry.

12	ounces skinless, boneless chicken breast halves
1	pound broccoli
½	cup chicken broth
2	tablespoons teriyaki sauce
2	teaspoons cornstarch
1	teaspoon toasted sesame oil
2	tablespoons cooking oil
1	tablespoon grated fresh ginger
1	clove garlic, minced
2	cups medium fresh mushrooms, halved or quartered
2	cups fresh bean sprouts (8 ounces)
1	red or green sweet pepper, cut into strips
1	8-ounce can sliced water chestnuts, drained
4	cups coarsely shredded lettuce (optional)

Cut chicken into 1-inch pieces. Remove florets from broccoli and cut in half (you should have about 3½ cups). Cut broccoli stalks into 1½-inch lengths; cut into ¼-inch strips (you should have about 1½ cups). Set aside.

For sauce, in a small bowl combine the chicken broth, teriyaki sauce, cornstarch, and sesame oil. Set aside.

Add cooking oil to a wok or 12-inch skillet. Preheat over medium-high heat (add more oil if necessary during cooking). Stir-fry ginger and garlic in hot oil for 15 seconds. Add the broccoli stems; stir-fry for 1 minute. Add broccoli florets; stir-fry for 2 to 3 minutes or until crisp-tender. Remove broccoli from wok.

Add mushrooms to wok; stir-fry about 1½ minutes or until crisp-tender. Remove from wok. Add bean sprouts and sweet pepper to wok; stir-fry for 1 to 2 minutes or until crisp-tender. Remove from wok. Add chicken to wok. Stir-fry for 3 to 4 minutes or until no longer pink. Push chicken from center of wok.

Stir sauce; add to center of wok. Cook and stir until thickened and bubbly. Return cooked vegetables to wok. Add water chestnuts. Stir all ingredients together to coat. Cook and stir about 2 minutes more or until heated through. If desired, spoon the chicken mixture over lettuce. Serve immediately. Makes 4 servings.

Nutrition information per serving: 261 cal., 11 g total fat (2 g sat. fat), 45 mg chol., 524 mg sodium, 19 g carbo., 24 g pro.

Chicken and Biscuit Pie

Nonfat dry milk powder makes a creamy gravy in this hearty one-dish meal.

1½ pounds chicken breast halves
2¼ cups water
1 bay leaf
2 cups cubed, peeled potatoes
    (2 medium)
1 cup chopped onion
½ cup nonfat dry milk powder
5 tablespoons all-purpose flour
1 teaspoon dried basil, crushed
¾ teaspoon poultry seasoning
¼ teaspoon salt
⅛ teaspoon pepper
1 cup frozen peas
    Green Onion Biscuits

Skin chicken. In a 4-quart Dutch oven combine chicken, water, and bay leaf. Bring to boiling; reduce heat. Cover and simmer for 20 to 25 minutes or until chicken is no longer pink (170°). Drain, reserving cooking liquid. Discard bay leaf. Cool chicken slightly. Cut chicken into bite-size pieces; discard bones.

Meanwhile, in a large saucepan cook potatoes and onion in a small amount of boiling water about 10 minutes or until potatoes are tender. Drain; return to saucepan. Cover and keep warm.

For sauce, in a small saucepan stir together the dry milk powder, flour, basil, poultry seasoning, salt, and pepper. Add 2 cups of the reserved cooking liquid, stirring until smooth. Cook and stir over medium heat until thickened and bubbly. Gently stir the sauce, cooked chicken, and peas into the potato mixture. Cover and keep warm while preparing Green Onion Biscuits.

Spoon chicken mixture into four 14-ounce individual casseroles or a 2-quart rectangular baking dish. Drop biscuit dough into 8 mounds onto the warm chicken mixture. Bake in a 400° oven for 20 to 25 minutes or until biscuits are golden brown and a wooden toothpick inserted into biscuits comes out clean. Makes 4 servings.

Green Onion Biscuits: In a small bowl stir together ⅔ cup all-purpose flour; 1 tablespoon thinly sliced green onion; 1 teaspoon baking powder; 1 teaspoon sugar; ¼ teaspoon dried basil, crushed; and dash salt. Combine ⅓ cup fat-free milk and 4 teaspoons cooking oil. Stir into flour mixture just until moistened.

Nutrition information per serving: 462 cal., 14 g total fat (3 g sat. fat), 61 mg chol., 315 mg sodium, 52 g carbo., 32 g pro.

Cincinnati-Style Chicken Chili

If desired, sprinkle this Midwestern favorite with freshly shredded cheddar cheese before serving.

1 **pound uncooked ground chicken or turkey**
1 **large onion, chopped**
1 **clove garlic, minced**
3 **tablespoons chili powder**
2 **teaspoons paprika**
1 **teaspoon ground cumin**
½ **teaspoon salt**
½ **teaspoon ground cinnamon**
⅛ **teaspoon ground cloves**
⅛ **teaspoon ground red pepper**
1 **bay leaf**
1 **14½-ounce can stewed tomatoes**
1 **8-ounce can tomato sauce**
½ **cup water**
1 **tablespoon red wine vinegar**
1 **tablespoon molasses**
1 **15-ounce can red kidney beans**
 Hot cooked spaghetti

In a 4½-quart Dutch oven cook ground chicken or turkey, onion, and garlic over medium heat for 5 to 7 minutes or until chicken is brown. Drain off fat, if necessary.

Add chili powder, paprika, cumin, salt, cinnamon, cloves, ground red pepper, and bay leaf. Cook and stir for 3 minutes.

Stir in undrained stewed tomatoes, tomato sauce, water, red wine vinegar, and molasses. Bring to boiling; reduce heat. Cover and simmer for 45 minutes, stirring occasionally. Uncover and simmer to desired consistency. Discard bay leaf.

In a medium saucepan heat undrained kidney beans; drain. To serve, spoon the chicken mixture and beans over hot cooked spaghetti. Makes 4 servings.

Nutrition information per serving: 402 cal., 8 g total fat (2 g sat. fat), 54 mg chol., 1,223 mg sodium, 61 g carbo., 30 g pro.

SERVING CINCINNATI-STYLE

Visit Cincinnati and you can sample chili that's unlike any you'll find in Texas or the Southwest. Cincinnati natives love their chili served over spaghetti or other pasta. They often sprinkle it with shredded cheese, chopped onion, and other toppers.

Cornish Hens with Basil-Wild Rice Stuffing

A combination of wild rice and basil makes for a nutty-tasting stuffing. The stuffing cooks in a handy foil packet on the grill.

1	tablespoon olive oil or cooking oil
¼	cup chopped onion
1	clove garlic, minced
2	cups cooked brown rice
1	cup cooked wild rice
¼	cup snipped fresh basil
2	tablespoons grated Parmesan cheese
½	teaspoon salt
	Dash ground nutmeg
2	1¼- to 1½-pound Cornish game hens
2	tablespoons honey
2	teaspoons Dijon-style mustard

For stuffing, in a large skillet heat oil over medium heat. Add onion and garlic; cook until onion is tender. Stir in brown rice, wild rice, basil, Parmesan cheese, salt, and nutmeg.

Fold a 36×18-inch piece of heavy foil in half to make an 18-inch square. Place stuffing in the center of the foil. Bring up two opposite edges of foil and seal with a double fold. Fold remaining ends to completely enclose the stuffing, leaving space for steam to build. Chill the packet until ready to grill.

Rinse Cornish hens; pat dry with paper towels. Twist wing tips under hens. Tie legs to tails. Insert an oven-going meat thermometer into center of an inside thigh muscle, not touching bone. In a small bowl stir together honey and mustard.

In a covered grill arrange medium-hot coals around a drip pan. Test for medium heat above the pan. Place hens, breast sides up, on grill rack over drip pan. Cover and grill for 50 to 60 minutes or until the thermometer registers 180°, brushing occasionally with mustard mixture the last 10 minutes of grilling. Meanwhile, place the foil packet of stuffing on grill rack directly over coals. Grill for 15 to 20 minutes or until heated through.

To serve, cut hens in half lengthwise with poultry shears. Serve with stuffing. Makes 4 servings.

Nutrition information per serving: 523 cal., 24 g total fat (5 g sat. fat), 102 mg chol., 470 mg sodium, 41 g carbo., 36 g pro.

Turkey Tenderloins with Honey-Lemon Sauce

In a hurry? These turkey tenderloins are ready in about 30 minutes. Make lighting the coals your first step—they'll need 20 to 30 minutes before they're ready for grilling.

1   large lemon
4   turkey breast tenderloin steaks
        (about 1 pound total)
⅓   cup water
3   tablespoons honey
1   tablespoon catsup
2   teaspoons cornstarch
1   teaspoon instant chicken bouillon
        granules
    Lemon wedges (optional)

Finely shred enough peel from the lemon to make 1 teaspoon. Cut lemon in half. Squeeze only one half to obtain 2 tablespoons juice; set peel and juice aside. Rub and squeeze remaining lemon half over turkey.

For sauce, in a small saucepan combine water, honey, catsup, cornstarch, bouillon granules, the 1 teaspoon lemon peel, and the 2 tablespoons lemon juice. Cook and stir over medium heat until mixture is thickened and bubbly. Cook and stir for 2 minutes more. Remove from heat. Cover and keep warm.

Place turkey on the rack of an uncovered grill directly over medium coals. Grill for 12 to 15 minutes or until turkey is no longer pink (170°), turning once.

(Or in a covered grill arrange medium-hot coals around a drip pan. Test for medium heat above the pan. Place turkey on grill rack over drip pan. Cover and grill for 15 to 18 minutes.)

Spoon the sauce over turkey. If desired, serve with lemon wedges. Makes 4 servings.

Nutrition information per serving: 175 cal., 2 g total fat (1 g sat. fat), 50 mg chol., 314 mg sodium, 16 g carbo., 22 g pro.

Curry-Glazed Turkey Thighs

Curry-Glazed Turkey Thighs

Turn economical turkey thighs into a company-pleasing entrée by glazing them with orange marmalade and dressing them with a yogurt sauce.

⅓ cup orange marmalade
1 tablespoon Dijon-style mustard
½ to 1 teaspoon curry powder
⅛ teaspoon salt
½ cup plain yogurt
2 small turkey thighs (about 2 pounds total)
Hot cooked rice (optional)
Raisins, peanuts, and/or chopped apple (optional)

For glaze, stir together marmalade, mustard, curry powder, and salt. For sauce, stir 3 tablespoons of the glaze into yogurt. Cover and chill until serving time. If desired, skin turkey. Insert an oven-going meat thermometer into center of a turkey thigh, not touching bone.

In a covered grill arrange medium-hot coals around a drip pan. Test for medium heat above the pan. Place turkey thighs on grill rack over drip pan. Cover and grill for 50 to 60 minutes or until the thermometer registers 180°, brushing once or twice with glaze the last 10 minutes of grilling. Slice turkey. Serve over hot cooked rice (if desired) and top with sauce. If desired, serve with raisins, peanuts, and/or apple. Makes 4 servings.

Nutrition information per serving: 157 cal., 4 g total fat (1 g sat. fat), 30 mg chol., 209 mg sodium, 21 g carbo., 9 g pro.

Turkey Parmigiana

Can't find turkey tenderloin steaks? Buy two whole turkey tenderloins and cut each in half horizontally to make four steaks.

8 ounces dried spaghetti
4 turkey breast tenderloin steaks (about 1 pound total)
1 tablespoon margarine or butter
2 tablespoons grated Parmesan cheese
1 14-ounce jar tomato and herb pasta sauce
¾ cup shredded mozzarella cheese (3 ounces)

Cook spaghetti according to package directions; drain. Cover and keep warm. Meanwhile, in a large skillet cook turkey in hot margarine or butter over medium heat for 8 to 10 minutes or until no longer pink (170°), turning once. Sprinkle with Parmesan cheese. Top with sauce. Cover and cook for 1 to 2 minutes or until heated through.

Sprinkle turkey with mozzarella cheese. Cover and let stand for 1 to 2 minutes or until cheese is melted. Serve with the hot cooked spaghetti. Makes 4 servings.

Nutrition information per serving: 518 cal., 12 g total fat (4 g sat. fat), 64 mg chol., 561 mg sodium, 62 g carbo., 37 g pro.

Turkey Tetrazzini

Tetrazzini is a quick supper when cooked in a wok—there's plenty of room for tossing the spaghetti with the turkey, mushrooms, and creamy sauce.

12	ounces turkey breast tenderloin
1⅔	cups milk
2	tablespoons all-purpose flour
2	teaspoons instant chicken bouillon granules
⅛	teaspoon pepper
¼	cup slivered almonds
1	tablespoon cooking oil
1	cup sliced fresh mushrooms
2	green onions, sliced (¼ cup)
2	tablespoons dry white wine, dry sherry, or milk
4	ounces dried thin spaghetti, cooked and drained
¼	cup finely shredded Parmesan cheese
2	tablespoons snipped fresh parsley
	Tomato slices (optional)
	Fresh parsley sprigs (optional)

Cut turkey into thin bite-size strips. For sauce, in a small bowl stir together the 1⅔ cups milk, the flour, chicken bouillon granules, and pepper. Set aside.

Preheat a wok or large skillet over medium-high heat. Stir-fry almonds in hot wok for 2 to 3 minutes or until golden brown. Remove almonds from wok. Let wok cool slightly.

Add cooking oil to cooled wok. Preheat over medium-high heat (add more oil if necessary during cooking). Stir-fry mushrooms and green onions in hot oil for 1 to 2 minutes or until tender. Remove the mushroom mixture from wok.

Add turkey to wok. Stir-fry for 2 to 3 minutes or until no longer pink. Push turkey from center of wok. Stir sauce; add to center of wok. Cook and stir until thickened and bubbly. Cook and stir for 2 minutes more.

Stir in wine, sherry, or milk. Return cooked mushroom mixture to wok. Add cooked spaghetti, Parmesan cheese, and the snipped parsley. Toss all ingredients together to coat. Cook and stir for 1 to 2 minutes more or until heated through. Sprinkle with toasted almonds. Serve immediately. If desired, garnish with tomato and parsley sprigs. Makes 4 servings.

Nutrition information per serving: 376 cal., 13 g total fat (4 g sat. fat), 50 mg chol., 637 mg sodium, 34 g carbo., 28 g pro.

Hot Turkey Sub Sandwich

Pair this hefty sandwich with bowls of tomato soup.

1	tablespoon olive oil
1	teaspoon dried basil, crushed
1	clove garlic, minced, or ⅛ teaspoon garlic powder
1	8-ounce loaf or ½ of a 16-ounce loaf French bread
6	ounces sliced mozzarella cheese
4	ounces sliced smoked turkey
2	tablespoons sliced pitted ripe olives
2	tomatoes, thinly sliced
⅛	teaspoon coarsely ground pepper

In a small bowl stir together the olive oil, basil, and garlic or garlic powder. Cut the French bread in half horizontally. Using a spoon, hollow out the top half, leaving a ¾-inch shell. Brush the cut sides of both bread halves with the olive oil mixture.

On the bottom half of the French bread, layer half of the mozzarella cheese, all of the smoked turkey, the olives, the remaining cheese, and the tomato slices. Sprinkle with pepper. Replace the bread top.

Wrap in heavy foil. Bake in a 375° oven about 10 minutes or until heated through. Cut into 4 serving-size portions. Makes 4 servings.

Nutrition information per serving: 335 cal., 13 g total fat (5 g sat. fat), 36 mg chol., 849 mg sodium, 33 g carbo., 22 g pro.

Parmesan-Turkey Sandwiches

Keep the ingredients you need for this sandwich on hand, and you'll be prepared every time your teenager invites friends for dinner.

1	slightly beaten egg
½	cup crushed cornflakes or rich round crackers
¼	cup grated Parmesan cheese
⅛	teaspoon garlic powder
⅛	teaspoon pepper
4	turkey breast tenderloin steaks (about 1 pound total)
2	tablespoons margarine or butter
4	lettuce leaves
4	hoagie buns, split and toasted
¼	cup bottled creamy Parmesan or buttermilk ranch salad dressing
2	tomatoes, thinly sliced

In a shallow dish beat together egg and 1 tablespoon water. In another shallow dish stir together crushed cornflakes or crackers, Parmesan cheese, garlic powder, and pepper. Dip turkey in egg mixture and roll in cornflake mixture to coat.

In a large skillet cook turkey in hot margarine or butter over medium heat for 8 to 10 minutes or until no longer pink (170°), turning once.

To assemble sandwiches, place lettuce on bottom halves of hoagie buns. Top with turkey, salad dressing, and tomato slices. Replace bun tops. Makes 4 servings.

Nutrition information per serving: 686 cal., 21 g total fat (5 g sat. fat), 112 mg chol., 1,177 mg sodium, 83 g carbo., 39 g pro.

Firecracker Turkey Burgers

Cool and creamy garlic sauce helps tame the fire brought on by spices and peppers in these smoky grilled patties.

½ cup mayonnaise or salad dressing
¼ cup dairy sour cream
1 clove garlic, minced
½ teaspoon cracked black pepper
¼ cup fine dry bread crumbs
2 tablespoons water
1 tablespoon chili powder
1 or 2 canned chipotle peppers in adobo sauce, drained and chopped (reserve 2 tablespoons adobo sauce)
2 cloves garlic, minced
¼ teaspoon salt
1 pound uncooked ground turkey or chicken
4 poppy seed rolls or hamburger buns, split and toasted
4 lettuce leaves
4 tomato slices
8 to 12 avocado slices (optional)

For sauce, in a small bowl stir together the mayonnaise or salad dressing, sour cream, the 1 clove garlic, and the black pepper. Cover and chill until serving time.

In a large bowl combine bread crumbs, water, chili powder, chipotle peppers, the 2 cloves garlic, and the salt. Add ground turkey or chicken; mix well. Form into four ¾-inch-thick patties.

Place patties on the rack of an uncovered grill directly over medium coals. Grill for 14 to 18 minutes or until done (165°), turning once.

To serve, spread the bottoms of rolls or buns with adobo sauce. Top with burgers and sauce. Add lettuce leaves, tomato slices, and, if desired, avocado slices. Replace roll or bun tops. Makes 4 servings.

Nutrition information per serving: 517 cal., 32 g total fat (8 g sat. fat), 111 mg chol., 700 mg sodium, 31 g carbo., 25 g pro.

Fish & SEAFOOD

Contents

Zesty Jalapeño Fish Fillets

Low in fat and full of flavor, this quick-to-fix recipe couldn't be easier.

---

1   pound fresh or frozen skinless red
    snapper, flounder, sole, haddock,
    or orange roughy fillets, ½ to
    1 inch thick
3   medium carrots, cut into thin
    bite-size strips (1½ cups)
1   medium zucchini, cut into thin
    bite-size strips (1½ cups)
1½ cups water
½   teaspoon instant chicken bouillon
    granules
1   cup quick-cooking couscous
⅓   cup jalapeño pepper jelly
1   tablespoon white wine vinegar or
    vinegar
1   tablespoon snipped fresh cilantro
    or parsley
    Fresh cilantro or parsley sprigs
    (optional)

Thaw fish, if frozen. Rinse fish; pat dry with paper towels. Cut fish into 4 serving-size portions. In a covered medium saucepan cook carrots in a small amount of boiling water for 2 minutes. Add zucchini and cook about 2 minutes more or until vegetables are crisp-tender; drain. Cover and keep warm.

Place fish on the greased unheated rack of a broiler pan. Sprinkle with salt and black pepper. Broil about 4 inches from the heat until fish flakes easily with a fork (allow 4 to 6 minutes per ½-inch thickness of fish). Turn 1-inch-thick fillets over halfway through broiling.

Meanwhile, in a small saucepan combine water and bouillon granules. Bring to boiling. Stir in couscous; remove from heat. Cover and let stand about 5 minutes or until liquid is absorbed.

In another small saucepan stir together jelly and vinegar. Heat and stir over low heat until jelly is melted.

To serve, fluff the couscous with a fork; stir in the snipped cilantro or parsley. Spoon the couscous onto dinner plates. Top with the fish and vegetables. Drizzle with the warm jelly mixture. If desired, garnish with cilantro or parsley sprigs. Makes 4 servings.

Nutrition information per serving: 320 cal., 2 g total fat (0 g sat. fat), 42 mg chol., 201 mg sodium, 44 g carbo., 30 g pro.

Sweet Pepper Salsa Fish

A garnish of fresh oregano complements the refreshing combination of sautéed vegetables and salsa topping.

1	**pound fresh or frozen skinless fish fillets, about ¾ inch thick**
2	**tablespoons cooking oil**
1½	**cups fresh mushrooms, quartered**
1	**cup coarsely chopped green and/or yellow sweet pepper**
1	**small onion, halved lengthwise and sliced**
1	**cup bottled salsa**
	Fresh oregano sprigs (optional)

Thaw fish, if frozen. Rinse fish; pat dry with paper towels. Cut fish into 4 serving-size portions; set aside.

In a large skillet heat 1 tablespoon of the oil over medium-high heat. Cook mushrooms, sweet pepper, and onion in the hot oil about 5 minutes or just until vegetables are tender. Remove vegetables with a slotted spoon; set aside.

Add the remaining 1 tablespoon cooking oil to skillet. Add fish. Cook over medium heat for 6 to 9 minutes or until fish flakes easily with a fork, turning once.

Spoon the cooked vegetables over fish. Top with salsa. Cover and cook over low heat about 2 minutes more or until heated through. If desired, garnish with fresh oregano. Makes 4 servings.

Nutrition information per serving: 190 cal., 10 g total fat (1 g sat. fat), 53 mg chol., 306 mg sodium, 8 g carbo., 21 g pro.

Storing fish

Sooner is better when it comes to cooking fish. If you're not going to cook it right away, wrap fresh fish loosely in plastic wrap, store it in the coldest part of the refrigerator, and use within 2 days. If you purchase frozen fish, keep it in a freezer set at 0° or lower for up to 3 months. If you cut your own fillets or steaks, put them in self-sealing freezer bags or wrap in moistureproof and vaporproof wrap before freezing.

Salmon with Apricot Sauce

Salmon contains the kind of fat that may protect against heart disease and some cancers. For a zap of extra flavor, the fish is topped with fruity hot pepper sauce.

4   fresh or frozen salmon or halibut steaks, cut ¾ inch thick (about 1¼ pounds total)
4   grilled fresh apricots or 8 dried apricots
½   cup apricot nectar
⅓   cup apricot preserves
3   tablespoons sliced green onions
1½ teaspoons snipped fresh oregano or ½ teaspoon dried oregano, crushed
⅛   teaspoon salt
    Few dashes bottled hot pepper sauce
1   tablespoon olive oil
1   to 2 teaspoons bottled hot pepper sauce
    Fresh oregano sprigs (optional)

Thaw fish, if frozen. Quarter grilled apricots; set aside. (Or cover dried apricots with boiling water. Let stand while preparing sauce. Drain well.)

For sauce, in a small saucepan combine apricot nectar, preserves, green onions, the snipped fresh or dried oregano, and the salt. Bring just to boiling, stirring frequently; reduce heat. Boil gently, uncovered, about 8 minutes or until sauce is slightly thickened. Remove from heat; reserve ¼ cup sauce to brush on fish. In a small bowl combine the remaining sauce, grilled or soaked apricots, and the few dashes hot pepper sauce. Cover and keep warm.

Rinse fish; pat dry with paper towels. In a small bowl stir together the olive oil and the 1 to 2 teaspoons hot pepper sauce. Brush both sides of fish with the oil mixture. Sprinkle with salt and black pepper.

Place fish on the greased rack of an uncovered grill directly over medium coals. Grill for 6 to 9 minutes or until fish flakes easily with a fork, turning once and brushing with the reserved ¼ cup sauce the last 2 to 3 minutes of grilling.

Arrange the fish on a serving platter. Spoon the sauce over fish. If desired, garnish with oregano sprigs. Makes 4 servings.

Nutrition information per serving: 304 cal., 8 g total fat (1 g sat. fat), 73 mg chol., 260 mg sodium, 27 g carbo., 29 g pro.

Fish à la Diable

If the fillets are small, overlap two or three to make one 4-ounce serving. If they're too large, cut them into serving-size portions.

4 4-ounce fresh or frozen croaker, mullet, flounder, whiting, turbot, or pollack fillets
2 medium carrots
1 cup sliced fresh mushrooms
⅓ cup sliced celery
½ cup plain yogurt
1 to 2 tablespoons Dijon-style mustard
½ of a medium red sweet pepper, cut into thin strips (½ cup)
½ of a medium green sweet pepper, cut into thin strips (½ cup)
1 tablespoon margarine or butter, melted
1 teaspoon all-purpose flour
3 tablespoons milk
   Fresh dill (optional)
   Lemon wedges (optional)

Thaw fish, if frozen. Rinse fish; pat dry with paper towels. Set aside.

Cut each carrot into 4 long strips (8 strips total). In a medium saucepan cook carrots, mushrooms, and celery in a small amount of boiling water about 5 minutes or until tender; drain. Separate carrots from mushrooms and celery; set vegetables aside.

In a small bowl combine the yogurt and mustard; set aside ⅓ cup of the mustard mixture. Brush the remaining mustard mixture over one side of each fillet. Place one-fourth of the red and green pepper strips and two carrot strips crosswise on mustard side of each fillet. Starting from a short end, roll up fish around vegetables.

Arrange fish rolls, seam sides down, in a 9×9×2-inch baking pan. Brush with melted margarine or butter. Bake in a 400° oven for 15 to 20 minutes or until fish flakes easily with a fork.

Meanwhile, for sauce, in a small saucepan stir flour into the reserved ⅓ cup mustard mixture; stir in milk. Add cooked mushrooms and celery. Cook and stir over medium heat until thickened and bubbly. Cook and stir for 1 minute more.

Transfer fish rolls to dinner plates. Spoon the sauce over fish. If desired, garnish with fresh dill and lemon wedges. Makes 4 servings.

Nutrition information per serving: 361 cal., 20 g total fat (5 g sat. fat), 107 mg chol., 630 mg sodium, 19 g carbo., 26 g pro.

Sesame Orange Roughy

To make onion brushes, slice roots from the end of each green onion and remove most of the upper, green portion. Slash the remaining green portion to make a fringe. Then place in ice water for a few minutes to curl the ends.

1 pound fresh or frozen orange roughy or other fish fillets, about ¾ inch thick
2 tablespoons lime or lemon juice
1 tablespoon margarine or butter
2 tablespoons water
4 teaspoons soy sauce
2 teaspoons honey
1 clove garlic, minced
½ teaspoon grated fresh ginger or ⅛ teaspoon ground ginger
½ teaspoon toasted sesame oil
½ teaspoon lime or lemon juice
¼ teaspoon pepper
1 green onion, sliced
2 teaspoons sesame seeds, toasted

Thaw fish, if frozen. Rinse fish; pat dry with paper towels. Cut fish into 4 serving-size portions. Brush both sides of fish with the 2 tablespoons lime or lemon juice.

In a large skillet cook fish in hot margarine or butter over medium heat for 6 to 9 minutes or until fish flakes easily with a fork, turning once. Transfer fish to dinner plates; cover and keep warm.

Meanwhile, in a small bowl combine water, soy sauce, honey, garlic, ginger, sesame oil, the ½ teaspoon juice, and the pepper. Carefully pour into skillet. Cook until heated through, scraping up any browned bits on bottom. Pour over fish. Sprinkle with green onion and sesame seeds. Makes 4 servings.

Nutrition information per serving: 269 cal., 5 g total fat (1 g sat. fat), 23 mg chol., 453 mg sodium, 33 g carbo., 21 g pro.

Thawing Fish

Your best bet for safety and quality is to thaw fish and shellfish slowly in the refrigerator. Place the unopened package of fish or shellfish in a container in the refrigerator and allow overnight thawing for a 1-pound package. If necessary, you can place the wrapped package under cold running water for 1 to 2 minutes to hasten thawing. Don't thaw fish or shellfish in warm water or at room temperature and do not refreeze fish; doing so is unsafe.

Fish Sandwich with Basil Mayonnaise

Baking these fillets at 500° results in a crumb coating that's nice and crispy. For crumb-topped fish (opposite), toss the crumb mixture with the margarine. Brush the fillets with milk and sprinkle the crumb mixture over the top of fillets before baking. Serve with or without the buns.

	Basil Mayonnaise
1	**pound fresh or frozen skinless fish fillets, about ½ inch thick**
¼	**cup milk**
½	**cup fine dry bread crumbs**
¼	**teaspoon paprika**
⅛	**teaspoon salt**
⅛	**teaspoon pepper**
2	**tablespoons margarine or butter, melted**
4	**hamburger buns or kaiser rolls, split and toasted**
	Shredded lettuce

Prepare Basil Mayonnaise. Cover and chill until serving time. Thaw fish, if frozen. Rinse fish; pat dry with paper towels. Cut the fish into 4 serving-size portions; set aside. Grease a shallow baking pan; set aside.

Pour milk into a shallow dish. In another shallow dish combine bread crumbs, paprika, salt, and pepper. Dip fish in milk and roll in crumb mixture to coat. Place fish in the prepared baking pan, tucking under any thin edges. Drizzle with melted margarine or butter.

Bake in a 500° oven for 4 to 6 minutes or until fish flakes easily with a fork and coating is golden brown. Serve fish in buns or rolls with lettuce and Basil Mayonnaise. Makes 4 servings.

Basil Mayonnaise: In a small bowl stir together 3 tablespoons mayonnaise or salad dressing; 2 tablespoons dairy sour cream; 2 tablespoons snipped fresh basil or ½ teaspoon dried basil, crushed; and ½ teaspoon finely shredded lemon peel.

Nutrition information per serving: 399 cal., 22 g total fat (5 g sat. fat), 30 mg chol., 529 mg sodium, 29 g carbo., 21 g pro.

Fish Creole

Firm-fleshed fish such as halibut, haddock, and orange roughy make excellent choices for this saucy rice combo.

1 pound fresh or frozen skinless, firm-fleshed fish fillets
1 medium onion, chopped (½ cup)
1 stalk celery, chopped (½ cup)
½ cup chopped green sweet pepper
2 cloves garlic, minced
2 tablespoons margarine or butter
1 14½-ounce can tomatoes, cut up
¼ cup water
2 tablespoons tomato paste
1 tablespoon snipped fresh parsley
1 teaspoon instant chicken bouillon granules
1 teaspoon chili powder
½ teaspoon Worcestershire sauce
Several dashes bottled hot pepper sauce
1 10-ounce package frozen cut okra
2 cups hot cooked rice
Lemon wedges (optional)

Thaw fish, if frozen. Rinse fish; pat dry with paper towels. Cut fish into 1-inch pieces; set aside.

In a large skillet cook onion, celery, sweet pepper, and garlic in hot margarine or butter until tender.

Stir the undrained tomatoes, water, tomato paste, parsley, bouillon granules, chili powder, Worcestershire sauce, and hot pepper sauce into onion mixture. Bring to boiling; reduce heat. Simmer, uncovered, for 5 minutes.

Add fish and okra to tomato mixture, stirring gently to mix. Return to boiling; reduce heat. Cover and simmer about 5 minutes or until fish flakes easily with a fork. Serve over hot cooked rice. If desired, serve with lemon wedges. Makes 4 servings.

Nutrition information per serving: 379 cal., 9 g total fat (2 g sat. fat), 36 mg chol., 626 mg sodium, 44 g carbo., 30 g pro.

Fish Kabobs with Coriander Rice

Instead of broiling, you can grill these spicy kabobs. Cook them on the greased rack of an uncovered grill directly over medium coals for 8 to 12 minutes and turn occasionally.

1½ pounds fresh or frozen halibut or
    sea bass steaks, cut 1 inch thick
¼ cup water
¼ cup lime juice
3 tablespoons snipped fresh parsley or
    1 teaspoon dried parsley flakes
2 tablespoons olive oil or cooking oil
1 clove garlic, minced
1 teaspoon ground cumin
    Dash black pepper
3 small zucchini and/or yellow
    summer squash, cut into
    ¾-inch slices (3 cups)
1 large red sweet pepper, cut into
    ¾-inch pieces
2 cups water
2 cloves garlic, minced
2 teaspoons ground coriander
1 teaspoon ground cumin
½ teaspoon salt
⅛ teaspoon crushed red pepper
1 cup uncooked long grain rice
⅓ cup sliced pitted ripe olives
3 tablespoons sliced green onions
    Lime slices, halved (optional)
    Thin red sweet pepper strips
    (optional)

Thaw fish, if frozen. Rinse fish; pat dry with paper towels. Cut fish into 1-inch cubes. Place fish in a plastic bag set in a shallow dish.

For marinade, in a small bowl combine the ¼ cup water, the lime juice, parsley, oil, the 1 clove garlic, 1 teaspoon cumin, and black pepper. Pour over fish; seal bag. Marinate at room temperature for 30 minutes, turning bag occasionally.

Meanwhile, in a medium saucepan cook zucchini and/or yellow squash and sweet pepper pieces in a small amount of boiling water for 2 to 3 minutes or just until crisp-tender. Drain.

For coriander rice, in another medium saucepan combine the 2 cups water, the 2 cloves garlic, the coriander, 1 teaspoon cumin, salt, and crushed red pepper. Bring to boiling. Stir in rice; reduce heat. Cover and simmer for 15 minutes. Remove from heat. Let stand, covered, about 5 minutes more or until liquid is absorbed. Stir in olives and green onions.

While rice is cooking, drain fish, reserving marinade. Alternately thread fish, zucchini and/or yellow squash, and sweet pepper pieces onto 12 metal skewers. Brush with the reserved marinade.

Place kabobs on the greased unheated rack of a broiler pan. Broil about 4 inches from the heat for 8 to 12 minutes or until fish flakes easily with a fork, turning once. Serve the kabobs with rice. If desired, garnish with lime slices and sweet pepper strips. Makes 6 servings.

Nutrition information per serving: 311 cal., 9 g total fat (1 g sat. fat), 36 mg chol., 285 mg sodium, 31 g carbo., 27 g pro.

Easy Salmon Pasta

To save time, cook the pasta and vegetables together in the same pan.

---

2 cups loose-pack frozen mixed vegetables or one 10-ounce package frozen mixed vegetables
1½ cups dried corkscrew pasta
2 green onions, sliced (¼ cup)
1 10¾-ounce can condensed cheddar cheese soup
½ cup milk
½ teaspoon dried dill
¼ teaspoon dry mustard
⅛ teaspoon pepper
2 6-ounce cans skinless, boneless salmon or tuna, drained
Fresh dill sprigs (optional)

In a large saucepan cook frozen mixed vegetables, corkscrew pasta, and green onions in boiling water for 10 to 12 minutes or just until pasta is tender. Drain well.

Stir soup, milk, dried dill, mustard, and pepper into pasta mixture. Gently fold in salmon or tuna. Cook over low heat until heated through. If desired, garnish with fresh dill. Makes 5 servings.

Nutrition information per serving: 347 cal., 9 g total fat (4 g sat. fat), 56 mg chol., 827 mg sodium, 41 g carbo., 22 g pro.

Hot Tuna Hoagies

This may be a sandwich, but you'll need a knife and fork to eat it.

1½ cups packaged shredded cabbage with carrot (coleslaw mix)
1 9¼-ounce can chunk white tuna (water pack), drained and broken into smaller chunks
2 tablespoons mayonnaise or salad dressing
2 tablespoons bottled buttermilk ranch, creamy cucumber, or creamy Parmesan salad dressing
2 hoagie buns, split and toasted
2 ounces cheddar or Swiss cheese, thinly sliced

In a medium bowl combine shredded cabbage with carrot and tuna. In a small bowl stir together mayonnaise or salad dressing and ranch, cucumber, or Parmesan salad dressing. Pour the mayonnaise mixture over tuna mixture; toss gently to coat.

Spread the tuna mixture on the hoagie bun halves. Place on the unheated rack of a broiler pan. Broil 4 to 5 inches from the heat for 2 to 3 minutes or until heated through. Top with cheese. Broil for 30 to 60 seconds more or until cheese is melted. Makes 4 servings.

Nutrition information per serving: 417 cal., 16 g total fat (5 g sat. fat), 40 mg chol., 788 mg sodium, 41 g carbo., 27 g pro.

Easy Salmon Pasta

Shrimp Piccata

Lemon, garlic, and white wine characterize this exceptionally easy, yet oh-so-elegant, entrée. Accompany the meal with crisp-tender stalks of steamed asparagus and garnish with scored lemon slices.

1	pound fresh or frozen, peeled and deveined large shrimp
2	tablespoons all-purpose flour
⅓	cup dry white wine
2	tablespoons lemon juice
1	tablespoon drained capers
¼	teaspoon salt
⅛	teaspoon pepper
1	tablespoon margarine or butter
2	cloves garlic, minced
2	cups hot cooked brown rice and/or wild rice
	Lemon slices, halved (optional)

Thaw shrimp, if frozen. Rinse shrimp; pat dry with paper towels. In a medium bowl toss shrimp with flour until coated. Set aside.

For sauce, in a small bowl stir together wine, lemon juice, capers, salt, and pepper. Set aside.

Place margarine or butter in a wok or large skillet. Preheat over medium-high heat until margarine is melted (add more margarine if necessary during cooking). Stir-fry garlic in hot margarine for 15 seconds.

Add half of the shrimp to wok. Stir-fry for 2 to 3 minutes or until shrimp turn opaque. Remove from wok. Repeat with the remaining shrimp. Remove all shrimp from wok.

Add sauce to wok. Cook and stir until sauce is bubbly and slightly reduced. Return shrimp to wok. Cook and stir about 1 minute more or until heated through.

Serve immediately over hot cooked brown and/or wild rice. If desired, garnish with lemon slices. Makes 4 servings.

Nutrition information per serving: 247 cal., 4 g total fat (1 g sat. fat), 174 mg chol., 405 mg sodium, 27 g carbo., 21 g pro.

Lemony Scampi Kabobs

To peel and devein the shrimp, use your fingers to open and remove the shell from the body to the base of the tail. Using a sharp knife, make a shallow slit along the center of the shrimp's back from the head end to the base of the tail. With the knife, remove the black sand vein.

1	pound fresh or frozen large shrimp in shells
2	small zucchini, cut into ¾-inch slices (2 cups)
1	large red sweet pepper, cut into 1-inch pieces (about 1½ cups)
1	clove garlic, minced
2	tablespoons margarine or butter
1	teaspoon finely shredded lemon peel
2	tablespoons lemon juice
¼	teaspoon ground red pepper
⅛	teaspoon salt
	Lemon wedges (optional)

Thaw shrimp, if frozen. Peel shrimp, leaving tails intact. Devein shrimp; rinse and pat dry with paper towels. Set aside.

In a small saucepan cook zucchini in a small amount of boiling, lightly salted water for 2 minutes; drain. Alternately thread shrimp, zucchini, and sweet pepper onto 8 metal skewers.

In a small saucepan cook garlic in hot margarine or butter until golden brown. Stir in lemon peel, lemon juice, ground red pepper, and salt. Set aside.

Place shrimp kabobs on the rack of an uncovered grill directly over medium coals. Grill for 8 to 10 minutes or until shrimp turn opaque, turning once and brushing occasionally with lemon mixture during the last half of grilling. If desired, serve the kabobs with lemon wedges. Makes 4 servings.

Nutrition information per serving: 134 cal., 7 g total fat (1 g sat. fat), 131 mg chol., 285 mg sodium, 4 g carbo., 15 g pro.

Stir-Fried Shrimp and Broccoli

This pleasing mixture of broccoli, carrots, and seasonings tastes equally delicious with shrimp or scallops. If you prefer, leave the tails on the shrimp for a striking presentation.

1	pound fresh or frozen medium shrimp in shells or 12 ounces fresh or frozen scallops
3	tablespoons red wine vinegar
3	tablespoons soy sauce
3	tablespoons water
1	tablespoon cornstarch
1½	teaspoons sugar
1	tablespoon cooking oil
2	cloves garlic, minced
2	cups broccoli florets
1	cup thinly bias-sliced carrots
1	small onion, halved lengthwise and sliced
1	cup sliced fresh mushrooms
2	cups hot cooked vermicelli, fusilli pasta, or rice

Thaw shrimp or scallops, if frozen. Peel and devein shrimp or cut any large scallops in half. Rinse the shrimp or scallops; pat dry with paper towels. Set aside.

For sauce, in a small bowl combine vinegar, soy sauce, water, cornstarch, and sugar; set aside.

Add oil to a wok or large skillet. Preheat over medium-high heat (add more oil if necessary during cooking). Stir-fry garlic in hot oil for 15 seconds. Add broccoli, carrots, and onion. Stir-fry for 3 minutes. Add mushrooms; stir-fry for 1 to 2 minutes more or until vegetables are crisp-tender. Remove vegetables from wok.

Stir sauce; add to wok. Bring to boiling. Add shrimp or scallops and cook for 2 to 3 minutes or until shrimp or scallops turn opaque. Return cooked vegetables to wok. Stir all ingredients together to coat. Heat through. Serve immediately with hot cooked pasta or rice. Makes 4 servings.

Nutrition information per serving: *395 cal., 6 g total fat (1 g sat. fat), 131 mg chol., 968 mg sodium, 62 g carbo., 26 g pro.*

Sea Shell Scallops

If you don't have plate-size coquille shells, use four individual au gratin dishes and alter the cooking method as follows: Bake the scallops in a 450° oven for 10 to 12 minutes or until opaque. Top the scallops with the sauce and sprinkle with the crumb mixture. Bake about 3 minutes more or until crumbs are golden brown.

1	pound fresh or frozen scallops
1	10-ounce package frozen chopped spinach
¼	cup shredded carrot
2	tablespoons thinly sliced green onion
2	tablespoons margarine or butter
3	tablespoons all-purpose flour
¼	teaspoon dried tarragon, crushed Dash pepper
1	cup chicken or vegetable broth
⅓	cup half-and-half, light cream, or milk
¼	cup fine dry bread crumbs
2	tablespoons grated Parmesan cheese
2	tablespoons margarine or butter, melted
	Shredded carrot (optional)

Thaw scallops, if frozen, and spinach. Cut any large scallops in half. Rinse scallops; pat dry with paper towels. Drain spinach well; divide evenly among 4 coquille shells. Arrange scallops in a single layer on spinach. Broil about 4 inches from the heat for 6 to 7 minutes or until scallops turn opaque.

Meanwhile, for sauce, in a small saucepan cook the ¼ cup shredded carrot and the green onion in the 2 tablespoons margarine or butter for 1 minute. Stir in flour, tarragon, and pepper. Add broth and half-and-half, light cream, or milk all at once. Cook and stir until thickened and bubbly. Cook and stir for 1 minute more. Spoon the sauce over scallops.

In a small bowl combine bread crumbs, Parmesan cheese, and the 2 tablespoons melted margarine or butter. Sprinkle over scallops and sauce. Broil about 2 minutes more or until crumbs are golden brown. If desired, sprinkle with additional shredded carrot. Makes 4 servings.

Nutrition information per serving: 286 cal., 16 g total fat (4 g sat. fat), 44 mg chol., 656 mg sodium, 15 g carbo., 21 g pro.

Pasta with Scallops and Fresh Vegetables

When sugar snap peas are out of season, substitute fresh Chinese pea pods that have been cut in half crosswise.

1 pound fresh or frozen sea scallops
8 ounces dried fettuccine or linguine
1 tablespoon margarine or butter
1 tablespoon cooking oil
2 or 3 cloves garlic, minced
2 large carrots, thinly bias-sliced (about 1½ cups)
2 cups fresh sugar snap peas, strings and tips removed
3 green onions, thinly sliced
½ cup dry white wine or chicken broth
⅓ cup water
1 tablespoon snipped fresh dill or 2 teaspoons snipped fresh tarragon
1 teaspoon instant chicken bouillon granules
¼ teaspoon crushed red pepper
2 tablespoons cornstarch
2 tablespoons cold water
Cracked black pepper
¼ cup grated Parmesan cheese

Thaw scallops, if frozen. Cut any large scallops in half. Rinse scallops; pat dry with paper towels. Set aside.

In a Dutch oven cook the pasta according to package directions; drain. Return pasta to Dutch oven; toss with margarine or butter. Cover and keep warm.

Meanwhile, add oil to a wok or large skillet. Preheat over medium-high heat (add more oil if necessary during cooking). Stir-fry garlic in hot oil for 15 seconds. Add carrots; stir-fry for 4 minutes. Add sugar snap peas and green onions; stir-fry for 2 to 3 minutes more or until vegetables are crisp-tender. Remove vegetables from wok. Cool wok for 1 minute.

Carefully add wine or chicken broth, the ⅓ cup water, the dill or tarragon, chicken bouillon granules, and crushed red pepper to wok. Bring to boiling. Add scallops; reduce heat. Simmer, uncovered, for 1 to 2 minutes or until scallops turn opaque, stirring occasionally.

Stir together cornstarch and the 2 tablespoons cold water; stir into scallop mixture. Cook and stir until thickened and bubbly. Return cooked vegetables to wok; add cooked pasta. Stir all ingredients together to coat. Heat through. Serve immediately. Sprinkle each serving with the cracked black pepper. Pass the Parmesan cheese. Makes 4 servings.

Nutrition information per serving: 462 cal., 10 g total fat (2 g sat. fat), 39 mg chol., 577 mg sodium, 60 g carbo., 27 g pro.

Crab Cakes

You know you're eating a great crab cake when chunks of meaty crab almost melt in your mouth. Accented with ingredients handpicked to bring out the crustacean's sweet and briny flavor, these cakes belong on your list of favorites.

1 6- to 8-ounce package frozen lump crabmeat or one 6-ounce can crabmeat, drained, flaked, and cartilage removed
1 slightly beaten egg
6 tablespoons fine dry bread crumbs
2 tablespoons finely chopped carrot
2 tablespoons finely chopped celery
2 tablespoons mayonnaise or salad dressing
1 tablespoon finely chopped green onion (green part only; reserve white part for Tartar Sauce)
¾ teaspoon dry mustard
¼ teaspoon salt*
¼ teaspoon bottled hot pepper sauce
2 tablespoons cooking oil
   Tartar Sauce
   Lemon wedges (optional)

Thaw crabmeat, if frozen. Drain. In a medium bowl combine the egg, 4 tablespoons of the bread crumbs, the carrot, celery, mayonnaise or salad dressing, green onion, dry mustard, salt, and hot pepper sauce. Gently stir in crabmeat just until combined. With wet hands, gently shape mixture into four ½-inch-thick patties.

Place the remaining bread crumbs in a shallow dish. Coat both sides of patties with crumbs. In a large skillet heat oil over medium heat. Add crab cakes. Cook about 6 minutes or until golden brown and heated through, turning once. Serve immediately with Tartar Sauce and, if desired, lemon wedges. Makes 4 servings.

Tartar Sauce: In a small bowl stir together ½ cup mayonnaise or salad dressing, 1 tablespoon chopped celery leaves, 1 tablespoon sweet or dill pickle relish, 1 tablespoon drained capers, and 1 tablespoon chopped green onion (white part only).

*****Note:** If using canned crabmeat, omit the ¼ teaspoon salt.

Nutrition information per serving: 298 cal., 26 g total fat (4 g sat. fat), 119 mg chol., 560 mg sodium, 7 g carbo., 11 g pro.

Buying Crabmeat

If you're making crab cakes, buy preshelled, cooked, or pasteurized lump crabmeat in 6- to 8-ounce containers. Or purchase crab in bulk—fresh, refrigerated, frozen, or canned. Thaw frozen crabmeat in the refrigerator for 1 or 2 days before using it. Thawing crabmeat under running water or in the microwave results in less flavor and dry meat. For unshelled crab, double the desired weight to allow for shell and cartilage.

Clam and Bacon Bundles

Brush the bundles with milk before you bake them; you'll be rewarded with a crispy, irresistibly golden brown crust.

2   slices bacon, cut up
¾   cup finely chopped broccoli
       (4 to 5 ounces)
1   medium carrot, shredded (½ cup)
1   small yellow summer squash,
       chopped (1 cup)
2   6½-ounce cans chopped clams,
       drained
⅓   of an 8-ounce tub (⅓ cup) cream
       cheese with chives and onion
2   tablespoons bottled creamy
       cucumber salad dressing
1   10-ounce package refrigerated
       pizza dough
1   tablespoon milk
1   tablespoon sesame seeds

In a large skillet cook bacon over medium heat until crisp. Drain bacon, reserving 1 tablespoon drippings in skillet. Set bacon aside.

For filling, add broccoli and carrot to the reserved drippings in skillet. Cook and stir for 2 minutes. Add squash; cook and stir for 1 minute more. Remove from heat. Stir in clams, cream cheese, cucumber salad dressing, and bacon.

Grease a baking sheet; set aside. On a lightly floured surface, roll pizza dough into a 12-inch square. Cut dough into four 6-inch squares. Place ½ cup of the filling on one corner of each square. Moisten edges and fold opposite corner over filling. Press edges with tines of a fork to seal. Brush bundles with milk. Sprinkle with sesame seeds.

Place bundles on the prepared baking sheet. Bake in a 400° oven about 20 minutes or until golden brown. Cool on a wire rack for 5 minutes. Serve warm. Makes 4 servings.

Nutrition information per serving: 390 cal., 18 g total fat (5 g sat. fat), 57 mg chol., 494 mg sodium, 35 g carbo., 23 g pro.

Meatless
DISHES

Contents

Mexican Black Bean Pizza

Hearty black beans flavored with cilantro top this meat-free pizza. Serve it with a crisp green salad.

1   10-ounce package refrigerated pizza dough

1   15-ounce can black beans, rinsed and drained

2   tablespoons snipped fresh cilantro or parsley

2   tablespoons bottled salsa

2   cloves garlic, quartered

1   teaspoon ground cumin

¼   teaspoon bottled hot pepper sauce

1½   cups shredded Colby-Monterey Jack cheese blend or cheddar cheese (6 ounces)

½   cup chopped red sweet pepper

¼   cup sliced green onions

½   cup dairy sour cream

2   tablespoons bottled salsa

Lightly grease an 11- to 13-inch pizza pan. Unroll the pizza dough and transfer to the prepared pan, pressing dough out with your hands. Build up the edges slightly. Prick generously with a fork. Bake in a 425° oven for 7 to 10 minutes or until light brown.

Meanwhile, in a blender container or food processor bowl combine black beans, cilantro or parsley, 2 tablespoons salsa, garlic, cumin, and hot pepper sauce. Cover and blend or process until smooth, stopping to scrape down sides, if necessary.

Spread bean mixture over hot crust. Sprinkle with cheese, sweet pepper, and green onions. Bake about 10 minutes more or until cheese is melted and pizza is heated through.

In a small bowl combine sour cream and 2 tablespoons salsa. Serve the pizza with sour cream mixture. Makes 4 servings.

Nutrition information per serving: 468 cal., 20 g total fat (11 g sat. fat), 50 mg chol., 917 mg sodium, 51 g carbo., 24 g pro.

℘IZZA DOUGH PRIMER

If you don't have refrigerated pizza dough on hand, or it's not available at your supermarket, you can prepare your own pizza dough for Mexican Black Bean Pizza (above). Use a favorite recipe or a store-bought mix. You'll need enough dough to fit an 11- to 13-inch pizza pan.

Hoppin' John with Grits Polenta

According to tradition, eating Hoppin' John on New Year's Day brings good luck. This appealing version has an Italian slant.

¾ cup uncooked long grain rice

½ of a 16-ounce package frozen black-eyed peas or one 15-ounce can black-eyed peas, rinsed and drained

1½ cups chopped red, yellow, and/or green sweet peppers

1 cup thinly bias-sliced carrots (2 medium)

1 cup frozen whole kernel corn

1 tablespoon finely chopped shallots or onion

4 cloves garlic, minced

2 teaspoons snipped fresh thyme or 1 teaspoon dried thyme, crushed

¼ teaspoon salt

¼ teaspoon crushed red pepper

⅛ teaspoon black pepper

2 teaspoons olive oil or cooking oil

2 medium tomatoes, seeded and chopped

2 tablespoons snipped fresh parsley
Grits Polenta
Fresh thyme sprigs (optional)

Cook the rice according to package directions, except omit any salt. If using frozen black-eyed peas, cook peas according to package directions; drain.

In a covered 12-inch skillet cook sweet peppers, carrots, corn, shallots or onion, garlic, snipped fresh or dried thyme, salt, crushed red pepper, and black pepper in hot oil for 6 to 8 minutes or until vegetables are crisp-tender, stirring occasionally.

Gently stir the cooked rice, black-eyed peas, and chopped tomatoes into vegetable mixture. Cover and cook over low heat about 5 minutes or until heated through, stirring occasionally. Stir in parsley. Serve with Grits Polenta. If desired, garnish with fresh thyme sprigs. Makes 6 servings.

Grits Polenta: In a medium saucepan combine 1⅓ cups water, ⅔ cup fat-free milk, and ⅛ teaspoon salt. Bring to boiling; reduce heat. Add ½ cup quick-cooking white (hominy) grits, stirring with a whisk. Cook and stir for 5 to 7 minutes or until very thick. Remove from heat. Add ½ cup shredded reduced-fat mozzarella cheese, stirring until melted. Coat a 9-inch pie plate with nonstick cooking spray. Spread grits mixture in pie plate. Cover and chill overnight. Cut firm grits into 12 wedges. Coat the unheated rack of a broiler pan with nonstick cooking spray. Arrange wedges on the prepared rack. Broil 4 to 5 inches from the heat for 4 to 5 minutes or until surface is slightly crisp and beginning to brown.

Nutrition information per serving: 295 cal., 4 g total fat (1 g sat. fat), 6 mg chol., 244 mg sodium, 54 g carbo., 12 g pro.

Tortilla-Black Bean Casserole

Reduced-fat dairy products make this family favorite more healthful. If desired, pass light sour cream, salsa, and sliced green onions as tasty toppers.

2	large onions, chopped
1½	cups chopped green sweet peppers
1	14½-ounce can tomatoes, cut up
¾	cup bottled picante sauce
2	teaspoons ground cumin
2	cloves garlic, minced
2	15-ounce cans black beans or red kidney beans, rinsed and drained
	Nonstick cooking spray
10	7-inch corn tortillas
2	cups shredded reduced-fat Monterey Jack cheese (8 ounces)
	Shredded lettuce (optional)
	Sliced small fresh red chile peppers (optional)

In a large skillet combine the onions, sweet peppers, undrained tomatoes, picante sauce, cumin, and garlic. Bring to boiling; reduce heat. Simmer, uncovered, for 10 minutes. Stir in the beans.

Coat a 2-quart rectangular baking dish with cooking spray. Spread one-third of the bean mixture over bottom of dish. Top with half of the tortillas, overlapping as necessary, and half of the cheese. Add another one-third of the bean mixture, then remaining tortillas and remaining bean mixture.

Cover and bake in a 350° oven for 35 to 40 minutes or until heated through. Sprinkle with the remaining cheese. Let stand for 10 minutes.

If desired, arrange the shredded lettuce on dinner plates. To serve, cut the casserole into squares and place on top of lettuce. If desired, garnish with chile peppers. Makes 6 to 8 servings.

Nutrition information per serving: 248 cal., 4 g total fat (1 g sat. fat), 0 mg chol., 631 mg sodium, 40 g carbo., 15 g pro.

Couscous with Beans and Carrots

Although couscous looks like a grain, it is actually tiny pasta. In Morocco, where couscous originated, it is prepared with a variety of vegetables and meats and is served in some form at almost every meal.

1   cup water
2   medium carrots, bias-sliced (1 cup)
1   medium onion, chopped (½ cup)
½   of a vegetable bouillon cube
       (enough for 1 cup broth)
1½   cups fresh pea pods, halved
       crosswise
1   15½-ounce can reduced-sodium
       garbanzo beans, rinsed and
       drained
1   cup quick-cooking couscous
½   cup fat-free milk
1   tablespoon snipped fresh savory or
       1 teaspoon dried savory, crushed
¼   teaspoon garlic powder
⅛   teaspoon pepper
½   cup shredded reduced-fat Monterey
       Jack cheese (2 ounces)

In a medium saucepan combine the water, carrots, onion, and vegetable bouillon cube. Bring to boiling; reduce heat. Cover and simmer for 6 minutes. Stir in the pea pods. Cover and simmer about 3 minutes more or until vegetables are crisp-tender.

Stir the garbanzo beans, couscous, milk, savory, garlic powder, and pepper into vegetable mixture. Bring just to boiling. Remove from heat. Cover and let stand for 5 minutes. Fluff with a fork. Sprinkle each serving with Monterey Jack cheese. Makes 4 servings.

Nutrition information per serving: 351 cal., 5 g total fat (2 g sat. fat), 11 mg chol., 468 mg sodium, 59 g carbo., 18 g pro.

Triple Mushroom and Rice Fajitas

This earthy three-mushroom filling paired with traditional fajita toppers makes a satisfying meatless meal. Substitute button mushrooms if you can't find the three suggested varieties in your supermarket.

½ cup uncooked regular brown rice
¼ cup water
2 tablespoons lime juice
1 tablespoon olive oil or cooking oil
2 large cloves garlic, minced
½ teaspoon ground cumin
½ teaspoon dried oregano, crushed
¼ teaspoon salt
3 ounces fresh portobello mushrooms, stemmed and thinly sliced
3 ounces fresh chanterelle or oyster mushrooms, thinly sliced
3 ounces fresh shiitake mushrooms, stemmed and thinly sliced
1 medium green and/or red sweet pepper, cut into thin strips
4 green onions, cut into 1½-inch pieces
8 7- to 8-inch flour tortillas
¼ cup slivered almonds, toasted
Green onion tops (optional)
Fresh cilantro (optional)

Cook brown rice according to package directions, except omit any salt.

Meanwhile, for marinade, in a large plastic bag set in a deep bowl combine the water, lime juice, oil, garlic, cumin, oregano, and salt. Add sliced mushrooms, sweet pepper strips, and green onion pieces; seal bag. Marinate at room temperature for 15 to 30 minutes, turning bag occasionally.

Stack tortillas; wrap in foil. Bake in a 350° oven about 10 minutes or until warm. (Or just before serving, microwave tortillas, covered with a paper towel, on 100% power [high] about 1 minute.)

For filling, in a large nonstick skillet cook undrained mushroom mixture over medium-high heat for 6 to 8 minutes or until pepper strips are tender and all but about 2 tablespoons of the liquid is evaporated, stirring occasionally. Stir in cooked brown rice and almonds; heat through.

To serve, spoon the mushroom mixture onto tortillas; roll up. If desired, tie a green onion top around each tortilla roll and garnish with cilantro. Makes 4 servings.

Nutrition information per serving: 331 cal., 9 g total fat (2 g sat. fat), 0 mg chol., 380 mg sodium, 55 g carbo., 9 g pro.

Risotto with Vegetables

Risotto (rih-ZOT-oh) is a classic Italian dish in which Arborio rice is first browned, then simmered in broth and constantly stirred so it absorbs the liquid. The finished product has a creamy consistency and a tender, but slightly firm, texture.

2   cups sliced fresh mushrooms
½   cup chopped onion (1 medium)
2   cloves garlic, minced
2   tablespoons olive oil or cooking oil
1   cup uncooked Arborio rice
3   cups vegetable or chicken broth
¾   cup asparagus or broccoli cut into bite-size pieces
¾   cup seeded and chopped tomato
¼   cup shredded carrot (1 small)
1   cup shredded fontina or Muenster cheese (4 ounces)
¼   cup grated Parmesan cheese
3   tablespoons snipped fresh basil or parsley
    Tomato slices (optional)

In a large saucepan cook mushrooms, onion, and garlic in hot oil until onion is tender. Add uncooked rice. Cook and stir over medium heat about 5 minutes or until rice is golden brown.

Meanwhile, in a medium saucepan bring broth to boiling; reduce heat and simmer. Slowly add 1 cup of the broth to the rice mixture, stirring constantly. Continue to cook and stir over medium heat until liquid is absorbed. Add another ½ cup of the broth and the asparagus or broccoli to rice mixture, stirring constantly. Continue to cook and stir until liquid is absorbed. Add another 1 cup broth, ½ cup at a time, stirring constantly until broth is absorbed. (This should take about 15 minutes total.)

Stir in the remaining ½ cup broth, the chopped tomato, and carrot. Cook and stir until rice is slightly creamy and just tender. Stir in fontina or Muenster cheese, Parmesan cheese, and basil or parsley. If desired, garnish with tomato slices. Makes 4 servings.

Nutrition information per serving: 406 cal., 19 g total fat (8 g sat. fat), 38 mg chol., 1,050 mg sodium, 48 g carbo., 16 g pro.

Zesty Vegetable Enchiladas

With melted cheese and tomato on top, these lentils and fresh vegetables wrapped in tortillas make a meal in themselves. (Pictured on front cover.)

1⅓ cups water
 ½ cup dry lentils, rinsed and drained
 8 6- or 7-inch flour tortillas
    Nonstick cooking spray
 2 medium carrots, thinly sliced
      (1 cup)
 1 medium zucchini or yellow summer
      squash, quartered lengthwise and
      sliced (2 cups)
 2 teaspoons chili powder or
      1 teaspoon ground cumin
 1 14½-ounce can chunky Mexican-
      style tomatoes
 1 cup shredded reduced-fat Monterey
      Jack cheese (4 ounces)
 ¼ teaspoon salt
    Dash bottled hot pepper sauce
      (optional)

In a medium saucepan combine water and lentils. Bring to boiling; reduce heat. Cover and simmer for 15 to 20 minutes or until tender. Drain lentils; set aside.

Meanwhile, stack tortillas; wrap in foil. Bake in a 350° oven about 10 minutes or until warm. (Or just before filling, microwave tortillas, covered with a paper towel, on 100% power [high] about 1 minute.) Coat a 2-quart rectangular baking dish with cooking spray; set aside.

Lightly coat a large skillet with cooking spray. Preheat over medium heat. Stir-fry carrots in hot skillet for 2 minutes. Add zucchini or yellow squash and chili powder or cumin. Stir-fry for 2 to 3 minutes or until vegetables are crisp-tender. Remove from heat. Stir in lentils, about half of the undrained tomatoes, ¾ cup of the cheese, the salt, and, if desired, hot pepper sauce.

Divide the vegetable mixture among warm tortillas; roll up tortillas. Place tortillas, seam sides down, in the prepared baking dish. Lightly coat tops of tortillas with cooking spray.

Bake in a 350° oven for 12 to 15 minutes or until enchiladas are heated through and tortillas are crisp.

Meanwhile, in a small saucepan heat the remaining undrained tomatoes. Spoon the tomatoes over enchiladas. Top with the remaining cheese. Makes 4 servings.

Nutrition information per serving: 401 cal., 10 g total fat (4 g sat. fat), 20 mg chol., 889 mg sodium, 58 g carbo., 21 g pro.

Roasted Red Pepper Sauce over Tortellini

Take advantage of ready-to-use roasted sweet peppers and refrigerated tortellini to speed up meal preparation. Then slow down and enjoy the delectable result.

1 **9-ounce package refrigerated cheese-filled tortellini**
1 **12-ounce jar roasted red sweet peppers, drained**
½ **cup chopped onion**
3 **cloves garlic, minced**
1 **tablespoon margarine or butter**
2 **teaspoons snipped fresh thyme or ½ teaspoon dried thyme, crushed**
2 **teaspoons snipped fresh oregano or ¼ teaspoon dried oregano, crushed**
1 **teaspoon sugar**

Cook the tortellini according to package directions; drain. Cover and keep warm.

Meanwhile, place roasted sweet peppers in a food processor bowl or blender container. Cover and process or blend until smooth. Set aside.

For sauce, in a medium saucepan cook the onion and garlic in hot margarine or butter until tender. Add the pureed roasted peppers, thyme, oregano, and sugar. Cook and stir until heated through. Pour sauce over cooked tortellini; toss gently to coat. Makes 3 servings.

Nutrition information per serving: 343 cal., 15 g total fat (4 g sat. fat), 75 mg chol., 298 mg sodium, 40 g carbo., 14 g pro.

KEEPING PASTA WARM

What do you do when the pasta is done, but the sauce has a few more minutes to cook? To keep the pasta warm without overcooking it, drain it in a metal colander. Then place the colander over a slightly smaller pot of boiling water (partially cover the colander with a lid). The steam from the water keeps the pasta warm and prevents it from drying out.

Lemony Alfredo-Style Fettuccine

Do you avoid pasta Alfredo because it's so high in fat? This luscious Alfredo-like sauce is made with reduced-fat cream cheese and evaporated fat-free milk to help keep the fat in check so you can indulge any time you like.

2 cups loose-pack frozen mixed
   vegetables
8 ounces dried spinach fettuccine or
   plain fettuccine
2 ounces reduced-fat cream cheese
   (Neufchâtel), cut up
½ cup evaporated fat-free milk
¼ cup grated Parmesan cheese
½ teaspoon finely shredded lemon peel
¼ teaspoon freshly ground pepper
   Dash ground nutmeg

Cook mixed vegetables according to package directions, except omit any salt; drain. Cover and keep warm.

Cook fettuccine according to package directions until tender but still firm, except omit any oil or salt; drain. Return fettuccine to saucepan.

Add cooked mixed vegetables, cream cheese, evaporated milk, Parmesan cheese, lemon peel, pepper, and nutmeg to cooked fettuccine. Heat through, tossing gently until cream cheese is melted and fettuccine is well coated. Serve immediately. Makes 4 servings.

Nutrition information per serving: 339 cal., 6 g total fat (4 g sat. fat), 17 mg chol., 256 mg sodium, 55 g carbo., 16 g pro.

COOKING WITH REDUCED-FAT CHEESES

Reduced-fat cheeses need a little extra care when it comes to cooking. Follow these tips for best results:
• Avoid boiling sauces and soups that use reduced-fat cheese; boiling causes the cheese to toughen.
• Shredding or cutting up reduced-fat cheese before adding it to heated mixtures induces melting more easily.
• When broiling or toasting cheese-topped dishes, remove them just as the cheese begins to melt.

Nutty Orzo and Vegetables

Check the pasta aisle carefully—tiny, rice-shaped orzo may be labeled rosamarina.

½ cup dried orzo pasta (rosamarina)
2 cups loose-pack frozen mixed vegetables
1 15-ounce can garbanzo beans, rinsed and drained
1 14½-ounce can low-sodium stewed tomatoes
1¼ cups bottled light spaghetti sauce
1 tablespoon snipped fresh thyme
¼ cup chopped cashews or slivered almonds, toasted
¼ cup shredded reduced-fat mozzarella cheese (1 ounce)
   Fresh thyme sprigs (optional)

In a large saucepan cook orzo according to package directions, except omit any salt. Add frozen mixed vegetables after 5 minutes of cooking. Drain. Return orzo mixture to saucepan.

Stir garbanzo beans, undrained tomatoes, spaghetti sauce, and the snipped thyme into cooked orzo mixture. Bring to boiling; reduce heat. Cover and simmer for 5 minutes.

Before serving, stir in toasted cashews or almonds. Spoon orzo mixture onto dinner plates or into serving bowls. Sprinkle each serving with mozzarella cheese. If desired, garnish with fresh thyme sprigs. Makes 4 servings.

Nutrition information per serving: 313 cal., 7 g total fat (2 g sat. fat), 4 mg chol., 364 mg sodium, 53 g carbo., 13 g pro.

*B*EAN WISDOM

Canned beans can save you time, but they also contribute sodium to your diet. A way to resolve this problem is to rinse the beans in a colander under running water and let them drain. You'll get great-tasting beans without the salty liquid that comes with them.

Pasta with Garden Vegetables

Two kinds of Italian cheese, Romano and provolone, combine with corkscrew pasta and an array of fresh vegetables to create a family favorite.

1	tablespoon cooking oil
1	clove garlic, minced
2	small zucchini, sliced ¼ inch thick (2 cups)
1	small yellow summer squash, sliced ¼ inch thick (1 cup)
2	cups sliced fresh mushrooms
⅓	cup sliced green onions
1	large tomato, chopped (1½ cups)
½	teaspoon dried oregano, crushed
⅛	teaspoon freshly ground pepper
8	ounces dried corkscrew pasta, cooked and drained
¼	cup finely shredded Romano or Parmesan cheese
1	cup shredded provolone or mozzarella cheese (4 ounces)

Add cooking oil to a wok or large skillet. Preheat over medium-high heat (add more oil if necessary during cooking). Stir-fry garlic in hot oil for 15 seconds.

Add zucchini and yellow squash; stir-fry for 3 minutes. Add mushrooms and green onions; stir-fry about 1 minute or until vegetables are crisp-tender. Add tomato, oregano, and pepper; stir-fry for 2 minutes more. Remove from heat.

Add the hot cooked pasta and the Romano or Parmesan cheese to vegetable mixture; toss to combine. Serve immediately. Sprinkle each serving with provolone or mozzarella cheese and additional pepper. Makes 4 servings.

Nutrition information per serving: 412 cal., 14 g total fat (7 g sat. fat), 27 mg chol., 340 mg sodium, 53 g carbo., 19 g pro.

Egg Ragout

This simple supper is the perfect conclusion to any weekend recreation, from a hike in the woods to a snooze on the couch. It's a scrumptious, creamy egg and vegetable mélange that makes the most of pantry staples.

1½ cups fresh sugar snap peas, strings and tips removed
1 cup baby sunburst squash, cut into quarters
4 green onions, thinly bias-sliced
4 teaspoons margarine or butter
2 tablespoons all-purpose flour
1¼ cups milk
2 tablespoons grated Parmesan cheese
1 teaspoon sweet-hot mustard or Dijon-style mustard
4 hard-cooked eggs,* coarsely chopped
4 bagels, split and toasted, or 4 slices whole wheat bread, toasted

In a covered medium saucepan cook sugar snap peas and sunburst squash in a small amount of boiling salted water for 2 to 4 minutes or until crisp-tender; drain.

In a large saucepan cook green onions in hot margarine or butter over medium heat until tender. Stir in flour. Add milk all at once. Cook and stir until thickened and bubbly. Stir in Parmesan cheese and mustard; add cooked vegetables. Cook and stir about 1 minute more or until heated through.

Gently stir eggs into vegetable mixture. Serve the egg mixture over toasted bagels or bread. Makes 4 servings.

*Note: To cook the eggs, place them in a medium saucepan. Add enough cold water to come 1 inch above the eggs. Bring to boiling; reduce heat. Cover and simmer for 15 minutes; drain. Run cold water over eggs or place eggs in ice water until cool enough to handle; drain. If desired, cover and chill up to 1 week. Peel eggs.

Nutrition information per serving: 392 cal., 13 g total fat (4 g sat. fat), 221 mg chol., 600 mg sodium, 49 g carbo., 19 g pro.

Vegetable Frittata

When you need a spur-of-the-moment meal, this egg dish saves the day. Serve it with sliced cucumbers, tossed in a light vinaigrette, and hearty bread.

1   cup water
1   cup broccoli florets
½   cup finely chopped carrot
    Nonstick cooking spray
¼   cup sliced green onions
¾   cup shredded reduced-fat cheddar
    or Swiss cheese (3 ounces)
2   8-ounce cartons refrigerated or
    frozen egg product, thawed
1   tablespoon snipped fresh basil or
    1 teaspoon dried basil, crushed
1   tablespoon Dijon-style mustard
¼   teaspoon pepper
    Tomato slices (optional)
    Fresh tarragon sprigs (optional)

In a medium saucepan combine the water, broccoli, and carrot. Bring to boiling; reduce heat. Cover and simmer for 6 to 8 minutes or until vegetables are crisp-tender. Drain well.

Coat a large nonstick skillet with cooking spray. Spread the cooked vegetables and green onions in bottom of skillet. Sprinkle with half of the cheese. In a medium bowl stir together the egg product, basil, mustard, and pepper. Pour over vegetables and cheese.

Cook over medium heat. As mixture sets, run a spatula around edge of skillet, lifting egg mixture so the uncooked portion flows underneath. Continue cooking and lifting the edge until egg mixture is nearly set (the surface will be moist). Remove from heat. Cover and let stand for 3 to 4 minutes or until top is set.

To serve, cut the frittata into wedges. Sprinkle with the remaining cheese. If desired, garnish with tomato slices and tarragon sprigs. Makes 8 servings.

Nutrition information per serving: 101 cal., 3 g total fat (1 g sat. fat), 6 mg chol., 287 mg sodium, 6 g carbo., 11 g pro.

Southwest Skillet

This stove-top main course is built on classic Southwestern favorites you can find in most supermarkets.

2   tablespoons sliced almonds
1   yellow sweet pepper, cut into thin
      bite-size strips
1   fresh jalapeño pepper, seeded and
      chopped
1   tablespoon olive oil or cooking oil
4   medium tomatoes (about
      1¼ pounds), peeled and chopped
1½   to 2 teaspoons purchased Mexican
      seasoning or Homemade Mexican
      Seasoning
¼   teaspoon salt
4   eggs
1   ripe medium avocado, seeded,
      peeled, and sliced (optional)
      Fresh chile peppers (optional)

In a large skillet cook almonds over medium heat for 4 to 5 minutes or until light brown, stirring occasionally. Remove from skillet; set aside. In the same skillet cook sweet pepper and jalapeño pepper in hot oil about 2 minutes or until peppers are tender. Stir in tomatoes, Mexican seasoning, and salt. Bring to boiling; reduce heat. Cover and simmer for 5 minutes.

Break one of the eggs into a measuring cup. Carefully slide the egg into the simmering tomato mixture. Repeat with remaining eggs. Sprinkle the eggs lightly with salt and black pepper.

Cover and cook eggs over medium-low heat for 3 to 5 minutes or until the whites are completely set and the yolks begin to thicken but are not firm.

To serve, transfer eggs to dinner plates with a slotted spoon. Stir tomato mixture; then spoon it around eggs on plates. Sprinkle with the toasted almonds. If desired, serve with avocado slices and garnish with chile peppers. Makes 4 servings.

Homemade Mexican Seasoning: In a small bowl stir together 1 to 1½ teaspoons chili powder and ½ teaspoon ground cumin.

Nutrition information per serving: 392 cal., 13 g total fat (4 g sat. fat), 221 mg chol., 600 mg sodium, 49 g carbo., 19 g pro.

Mandarin Tofu Stir-Fry

Tofu takes on whatever flavors you mix with it. In this case a sweet-and-sour sauce does the trick.

½ cup bottled sweet-and-sour sauce
⅛ teaspoon ground red pepper
1 tablespoon cooking oil
6 green onions, bias-sliced into 1-inch
   pieces (1 cup)
½ of a medium red or green sweet
   pepper, cut into thin strips
2 cups fresh pea pods or one 6-ounce
   package frozen pea pods, thawed
1 16-ounce package extra-firm tofu
   (fresh bean curd), well drained
   and cut into ¾-inch cubes
1 11-ounce can mandarin orange
   sections, drained, or 3 medium
   oranges, peeled and sectioned
2 cups hot cooked rice
2 tablespoons unsalted dry roasted
   peanuts

For sauce, in a small bowl stir together sweet-and-sour sauce and ground red pepper. Set aside.

Add cooking oil to a wok or large skillet. Preheat over medium-high heat (add more oil if necessary during cooking). Stir-fry green onions and sweet pepper in hot oil for 1 minute. If using fresh pea pods, add to wok. Stir-fry for 1 to 2 minutes more or until vegetables are crisp-tender. Push vegetables from center of wok.

Add sauce to center of wok. Cook and stir until bubbly. Add tofu, orange sections, and, if using, thawed frozen pea pods. Gently stir all ingredients together to coat. Cover and cook for 1 to 2 minutes more or until heated through.

Serve immediately with hot cooked rice. Sprinkle with peanuts. Makes 4 servings.

Nutrition information per serving: 360 cal., 12 g total fat (2 g sat. fat), 0 mg chol., 117 mg sodium, 53 g carbo., 15 g pro.

TOFU TIPS

A process similar to the one used for making cheese transforms soybean milk into soybean curd, also called tofu. Tofu is sold in blocks or cakes and comes in soft, firm, and extra-firm varieties. Extra-firm tofu is recommended for stir-fried dishes because it holds its shape well. Look for it in the refrigerated area of your supermarket produce section.

Tofu Pitas with Mango Salsa

Although the ingredients for Jamaican jerk seasoning differ from brand to brand, this Caribbean blend typically includes chile peppers, thyme, and spices. Look for it in the seasoning aisle of your supermarket.

2 tablespoons lime juice or lemon juice
1 teaspoon cooking oil
½ teaspoon purchased Jamaican jerk seasoning or Homemade Jamaican Jerk Seasoning (recipe, page 101)
1 10½-ounce package extra-firm light tofu (fresh bean curd)
Nonstick cooking spray
⅓ cup quick-cooking couscous
Mango Salsa
3 large pita bread rounds, halved crosswise
Spinach leaves or torn lettuce leaves
Lime slices (optional)
Fresh thyme or marjoram sprigs (optional)

For marinade, in a shallow dish or pie plate combine the lime or lemon juice, oil, and Jamaican jerk seasoning. Cut tofu into ½-inch slices. Add tofu slices to marinade and brush marinade over slices. Cover and marinate at room temperature for 30 minutes, turning slices once and brushing with marinade. (Or cover and marinate in the refrigerator up to 6 hours, turning and brushing slices occasionally with marinade.)

Coat a grill basket with cooking spray. Place tofu slices in prepared grill basket. Discard marinade. Place basket with tofu slices on the rack of an uncovered grill directly over medium-hot coals. Grill about 10 minutes or until heated through, turning once. (Or coat the unheated rack of a broiler pan with cooking spray. Place tofu on prepared rack. Broil 5 to 6 inches from the heat about 8 minutes, turning once.) Cut the tofu slices into cubes.

Meanwhile, cook couscous according to package directions, except omit any butter or salt.

To serve, add tofu cubes and cooked couscous to Mango Salsa; toss gently to combine. Line pita halves with spinach or lettuce leaves. Spoon the tofu mixture into pita halves. If desired, garnish with lime slices and fresh thyme or marjoram. Makes 6 servings.

Mango Salsa: In a medium bowl combine 1 cup peeled and chopped mango; 1 small tomato, seeded and chopped; ½ of a medium cucumber, seeded and chopped; 1 thinly sliced green onion; 2 tablespoons snipped fresh cilantro; 1 fresh jalapeño pepper, seeded and chopped; and 1 tablespoon lime or lemon juice. Cover and chill until serving time. Makes about 2 cups.

Nutrition information per serving: 179 cal., 2 g total fat (0 g sat. fat), 0 mg chol., 251 mg sodium, 32 g carbo., 9 g pro.

Roasted Vegetable Medley with Rice

Roasting the potatoes, carrots, and fennel in a marjoram, vinegar, and oil dressing gives them a robust oven-browned flavor.

Nonstick cooking spray
12 ounces tiny new potatoes, quartered
4 medium carrots, thinly bias-sliced
1 small fennel bulb, halved lengthwise and thinly sliced
⅓ cup vinegar
1 tablespoon water
1 tablespoon olive oil or cooking oil
2 teaspoons snipped fresh marjoram or ½ teaspoon dried marjoram, crushed
1½ teaspoons sugar
½ teaspoon celery seeds
⅛ teaspoon garlic powder
1 15½-ounce can reduced-sodium garbanzo beans, rinsed and drained
2 cups water
1 vegetable bouillon cube (enough for 2 cups broth)
1 cup uncooked jasmine rice or long grain rice
Leafy fennel tops (optional)

Coat a 15×10×1-inch baking pan with cooking spray. In the prepared baking pan combine the potatoes, carrots, and fennel. In a small bowl combine vinegar, the 1 tablespoon water, the oil, marjoram, sugar, celery seeds, and garlic powder. Pour over vegetables; toss to coat.

Roast in a 450° oven for 35 minutes, stirring once. Add garbanzo beans, tossing to combine. Roast about 5 minutes more or until vegetables are tender and beans are heated through.

Meanwhile, in a small saucepan combine the 2 cups water and the bouillon cube. Bring to boiling. Stir in uncooked rice; reduce heat. Cover and cook for 15 to 20 minutes or until rice is tender and liquid is absorbed.

To serve, fluff cooked rice with a fork. Serve the roasted vegetables with the hot cooked rice. If desired, garnish with leafy fennel tops. Makes 4 servings.

Nutrition information per serving: 411 cal., 6 g total fat (1 g sat. fat), 0 mg chol., 499 mg sodium, 81 g carbo., 11 g pro.

Fettuccine with Grilled Vegetables

If you're using wooden skewers, soak them in water for about 30 minutes to prevent them from burning on the hot grill. For an eye-catching presentation, arrange the grilled vegetables over a combination of plain and spinach fettuccine.

1 small eggplant, peeled and cut into 1-inch pieces
2 large fresh portobello mushrooms, stemmed and cut into 1½-inch pieces
1 large green sweet pepper, cut into 1-inch pieces
½ cup dry white wine
¼ cup water
1 vegetable bouillon cube (enough for 2 cups broth)
1 tablespoon cornstarch
1 tablespoon snipped fresh basil or 1 teaspoon dried basil, crushed
2 teaspoons snipped fresh savory or ½ teaspoon dried savory, crushed
2 teaspoons snipped fresh thyme or ½ teaspoon dried thyme, crushed
8 ounces dried spinach fettuccine or plain fettuccine
1 small tomato, chopped (½ cup)
½ cup shredded reduced-fat mozzarella cheese (2 ounces)
2 tablespoons finely shredded Parmesan cheese
¼ teaspoon freshly ground black pepper

Thread the eggplant, mushroom, and sweet pepper pieces alternately onto eight 12-inch skewers; set aside.

For sauce, in a small saucepan combine wine, water, bouillon cube, cornstarch, basil, savory, and thyme. Cook and stir until thickened and bubbly. Cook and stir for 1 minute more. Brush kabobs with 1 to 2 tablespoons of the sauce. Cover remaining sauce and keep warm.

Place kabobs on the rack of an uncovered grill directly over medium coals. Grill for 8 to 10 minutes or just until vegetables are tender, turning once. (Or place kabobs on the greased unheated rack of a broiler pan. Broil 3 to 4 inches from the heat for 8 to 10 minutes, turning once.)

Meanwhile, cook pasta according to package directions, except omit any oil or salt; drain. Cover and keep warm.

To serve, toss the cooked pasta with the remaining sauce and arrange on dinner plates. Slide the vegetables from skewers onto pasta. Sprinkle with tomato, mozzarella cheese, Parmesan cheese, and black pepper. Makes 4 servings.

Nutrition information per serving: 354 cal., 5 g total fat (2 g sat. fat), 10 mg chol., 583 mg sodium, 58 g carbo., 16 g pro.

Eggplant Parmigiana

In this healthful version of eggplant parmigiana, the fat content is minimized by parboiling the eggplant and zucchini instead of frying them and by using reduced-fat cheeses.

1   medium eggplant (about 1 pound)
2   cups zucchini bias-sliced about
     ¼ inch thick
¼   teaspoon salt
1   cup light ricotta cheese or low-fat
     cottage cheese, drained
1   15-ounce container refrigerated
     fat-free vegetable marinara sauce
     or 2 cups bottled light spaghetti
     sauce
1   small tomato, thinly sliced
½   cup shredded reduced-fat mozzarella
     cheese (2 ounces)
2   tablespoons grated Parmesan cheese

If desired, peel eggplant. Cut eggplant into ½-inch slices; halve each slice. In a large saucepan cook the eggplant, zucchini, and salt in a small amount of boiling water for 4 minutes. Drain vegetables; pat dry with paper towels.

Divide the eggplant and zucchini among 4 individual au gratin dishes or casseroles. Top with the ricotta or cottage cheese. Spoon the marinara sauce or spaghetti sauce over cheese and top with sliced tomato. Sprinkle with the mozzarella cheese and Parmesan cheese.

Bake in a 350° oven for 20 to 25 minutes or until heated through. Makes 4 servings.

Nutrition information per serving: 212 cal., 6 g total fat (3 g sat. fat), 21 mg chol., 560 mg sodium, 27 g carbo., 15 g pro.

ℰGGPLANT—A PERENNIAL FAVORITE

Popular dishes such as Eggplant Parmigiana (above) rely on the dark purple, pear-shape eggplant. There are several types of eggplant available, including western, white, Japanese, and small (baby) eggplant. When selecting one, look for a plump, glossy, heavy fruit. Don't buy one that's scarred, bruised, or has dull skin. Its green stem cap should be fresh looking and free of mold. You can refrigerate an eggplant up to 2 days before using.

Garden Veggie Burgers

Two toppings—sharp red onion and a tangy spinach-feta combination—add zest to these grilled meatless burgers.

2   medium red onions
¼   cup bottled vinaigrette salad
       dressing (room temperature)
4   refrigerated or frozen meatless
       burger patties
4   cups spinach leaves
1   clove garlic, minced
1   tablespoon olive oil
½   cup crumbled feta cheese (2 ounces)
4   hamburger buns

For onion topping, cut onions into ½-inch slices. Place onions on the rack of an uncovered grill directly over medium coals. Grill for 15 to 20 minutes or until tender, turning once and brushing occasionally with salad dressing. Add the meatless patties to grill alongside onions; grill for 8 to 10 minutes or until heated through, turning once.

For spinach topping, in a large skillet cook and stir the spinach and garlic in hot olive oil over medium-high heat about 30 seconds or just until spinach is wilted. Remove from heat. Stir in the feta cheese.

To serve, place onion slices on bottoms of buns. Top with the grilled burgers, spinach topping, and bun tops. Makes 4 servings.

Nutrition information per serving: 350 cal., 14 g total fat (4 g sat. fat), 17 mg chol., 920 mg sodium, 37 g carbo., 21 g pro.

Cookies
& CAKES

Contents

Fruit Chip Cookies

Everyone in the family will find something to love about these tender morsels packed with dried fruit, hazelnuts, granola, and white baking pieces.

1   cup butter
¾   cup packed brown sugar
½   cup granulated sugar
1   teaspoon baking soda
2   eggs
1   teaspoon vanilla
1⅔ cups all-purpose flour
2   cups granola cereal
1   6-ounce package mixed dried
      fruit bits
1   cup chopped hazelnuts (filberts)
      or walnuts
1   cup white baking pieces

In a large mixing bowl beat butter with an electric mixer on medium to high speed for 30 seconds. Add brown sugar, granulated sugar, and soda; beat until combined. Beat in eggs and vanilla until combined.

Beat in as much of the flour as you can with the mixer. Stir in any remaining flour and the granola with a wooden spoon. Stir in dried fruit bits, nuts, and white baking pieces.

Drop dough by a slightly rounded tablespoon about 2 inches apart onto an ungreased cookie sheet. Flatten slightly.

Bake in a 325° oven for 11 to 13 minutes or until edges are brown. Cool on cookie sheet for 1 minute. Transfer cookies to a wire rack; cool. Makes about 48 cookies.

Nutrition information per cookie: 137 cal., 7 g total fat (4 g sat. fat), 21 mg chol., 86 mg sodium, 17 g carbo., 2 g pro.

DROP COOKIE CLUES

For attractive drop cookies, use a spoon from your flatware set—not a measuring spoon—to drop them, making the mounds the same size and spacing them evenly on the cookie sheet. Don't crowd the mounds. When a recipe calls for a greased cookie sheet, use only a light coating of shortening. A heavy coating causes the cookies to spread too much. And don't drop the dough onto a hot cookie sheet. The heat causes the cookies to flatten. Instead use two cookie sheets or allow your one sheet to cool between batches.

Browned Butter Cookies and Pecan Drops (recipe, page 228)

Browned Butter Cookies

The French term for browned butter is "beurre noisette," referring to butter that's cooked to a light hazelnut color. Coincidentally, browned butter has a nutty flavor too.

½ cup butter
1½ cups packed brown sugar
1 teaspoon baking soda
½ teaspoon baking powder
¼ teaspoon salt
2 eggs
1 teaspoon vanilla
2½ cups all-purpose flour
1 8-ounce carton dairy sour cream
1 cup coarsely chopped walnuts
Browned Butter Icing

Grease a cookie sheet; set aside. In a large mixing bowl beat butter with an electric mixer on medium to high speed for 30 seconds. Add brown sugar, baking soda, baking powder, and salt; beat until combined. Beat in eggs and vanilla until fluffy.

Beat in as much of the flour as you can with the mixer. Stir in any remaining flour and the sour cream with a wooden spoon. Stir in coarsely chopped walnuts.

Drop dough by a rounded teaspoon about 2 inches apart onto the prepared cookie sheet.

Bake in a 350° oven about 10 minutes or until set. Transfer cookies to a wire rack; cool. Frost cookies with Browned Butter Icing. Makes about 56 cookies.

Browned Butter Icing: In a medium saucepan heat ¼ cup butter over medium heat until butter turns the color of light brown sugar. Remove from heat. Stir in 2 cups sifted powdered sugar and enough boiling water (1 to 2 tablespoons) to make an icing of spreading consistency. Frost cooled cookies immediately after preparing frosting. If the frosting becomes grainy, soften with a few drops of hot water.

Nutrition information per cookie: 97 cal., 5 g total fat (2 g sat. fat), 16 mg chol., 66 mg sodium, 13 g carbo., 1 g pro.

Pecan Drops

Select the nicest pecan halves for the cookie tops and chop the rest before stirring them into the dough. (Pictured on page 226.)

½ cup butter
2 cups sifted powdered sugar
1¾ cups all-purpose flour
⅓ cup milk
1 egg
1 teaspoon baking powder
1 teaspoon vanilla
1 cup coarsely chopped pecans
Granulated sugar
Pecan halves (optional)

Lightly grease a cookie sheet; set aside. In a large mixing bowl beat the butter with an electric mixer on medium to high speed for 30 seconds.

Add powdered sugar, about half of the flour, half of the milk, the egg, baking powder, and vanilla. Beat until combined. Beat or stir in the remaining flour and the remaining milk. Stir in chopped pecans.

Drop dough by a rounded teaspoon about 2 inches apart onto the prepared cookie sheet. Sprinkle with granulated sugar. If desired, lightly press a pecan half in the center of each cookie.

Bake in a 375° oven for 8 to 10 minutes or until edges are light brown. Transfer the cookies to a wire rack; cool. Makes about 36 cookies.

Nutrition information per cookie: 90 cal., 5 g total fat (1 g sat. fat), 9 mg chol., 36 mg sodium, 11 g carbo., 1 g pro.

Fudge Ecstasies

You'll think you broke the chocolate bank when you bite into one of these chewy, double-chocolate, nut-filled wonders.

1   12-ounce package (2 cups) semisweet chocolate pieces
2   ounces unsweetened chocolate, chopped
2   tablespoons butter
2   eggs
⅔   cup sugar
¼   cup all-purpose flour
1   teaspoon vanilla
¼   teaspoon baking powder
1   cup chopped nuts

Grease a cookie sheet; set aside. In a heavy medium saucepan combine 1 cup of the chocolate pieces, the unsweetened chocolate, and butter. Cook and stir over medium-low heat until melted. Remove from heat.

Add the eggs, sugar, flour, vanilla, and baking powder. Beat until combined, scraping sides of pan occasionally. Stir in the remaining chocolate pieces and the nuts.

Drop dough by a rounded teaspoon about 2 inches apart onto the prepared cookie sheet.

Bake in a 350° oven for 8 to 10 minutes or until edges are firm and surfaces are dull and slightly cracked. Transfer cookies to a wire rack; cool. Makes about 36 cookies.

Nutrition information per cookie: 101 cal., 6 g total fat (1 g sat. fat), 14 mg chol., 13 mg sodium, 12 g carbo., 2 g pro.

Better with Butter

All of the cookie recipes in this book call for butter. Butter lends its wonderful flavor and ensures good results. Many margarines contain more water than oil and yield undesirable results. If you wish to use margarine instead of butter, use only stick margarine that contains at least 80% vegetable oil (oil content is listed on the package). Margarines produce a softer dough, so you may need to chill it longer than directed. Soft, spreadable margarines have a high water content and often result in tough cookies that dry out faster.

Best-Ever Bourbon Brownies

The unusual addition of bourbon gives ever-popular brownies a distinctive flavor. If you prefer to cook without alcohol, simply omit the first drizzling step.

½ cup granulated sugar
⅓ cup butter
2 tablespoons water
1 cup semisweet chocolate pieces
2 eggs
1 teaspoon vanilla
¾ cup all-purpose flour
¼ teaspoon baking soda
¼ teaspoon salt
½ cup chopped pecans
2 to 3 tablespoons bourbon
   Butter Frosting
1 ounce semisweet chocolate, melted

Grease an 8×8×2-inch baking pan; set aside. In a medium saucepan combine granulated sugar, butter, and water. Cook and stir over medium heat just until mixture boils. Remove from heat. Add chocolate pieces, stirring until melted. Add eggs and vanilla, beating with a wooden spoon just until combined.

Combine flour, baking soda, and salt. Stir flour mixture and pecans into chocolate mixture. Spread batter in the prepared pan.

Bake in a 350° oven about 20 minutes or until edges are set and begin to pull away from sides of pan.

Using a fork, prick the warm brownies several times. Drizzle bourbon evenly over brownies. Cool in pan on a wire rack.

Spread Butter Frosting over brownies; drizzle with melted chocolate. Cut into bars. Makes 16 to 20 brownies.

Butter Frosting: In a small mixing bowl beat 3 tablespoons butter with an electric mixer on medium to high speed for 30 seconds. Gradually add 1½ cups sifted powdered sugar, beating well. Slowly beat in 2 teaspoons milk and ¼ teaspoon vanilla. If necessary, beat in enough additional milk to make a frosting of spreading consistency.

Nutrition information per brownie: 235 cal., 13 g total fat (6 g sat. fat), 44 mg chol., 129 mg sodium, 24 g carbo., 2 g pro.

Top-of-the-World Brownies

You can't possibly resist these chewy fudge-nut brownies. Each wears a billowing thunderhead of crisp chocolate meringue.

¾ cup butter
3 ounces unsweetened chocolate, coarsely chopped
1⅓ cups sugar
2 teaspoons vanilla
3 eggs
1 cup all-purpose flour
2 tablespoons unsweetened cocoa powder
½ cup coarsely chopped hazelnuts (filberts) or pecans
2 egg whites
⅔ cup sugar
1 tablespoon unsweetened cocoa powder

Line the bottom and sides of an 8×8×2-inch baking pan with heavy foil; grease the foil. Set pan aside.

In a medium saucepan cook and stir the ¾ cup butter and the unsweetened chocolate over low heat just until melted. Remove from heat. Using a wooden spoon, stir in the 1⅓ cups sugar and the vanilla. Cool about 5 minutes.

Add eggs, one at a time, beating just until combined after each addition. Stir in flour and the 2 tablespoons cocoa powder. Spread batter evenly in prepared pan. Sprinkle with nuts; set aside.

For meringue, in a small mixing bowl beat the egg whites with an electric mixer on medium to high speed about 1 minute or until soft peaks form (tips curl). Gradually add the ⅔ cup sugar, beating on high speed until stiff peaks form (tips stand straight) and sugar is almost dissolved. Reduce speed to low; beat in the 1 tablespoon cocoa powder. Using a tablespoon, carefully spoon the meringue in 16 even mounds on top of the brownie batter, keeping about ½ inch of space between each mound.

Bake in a 350° oven about 1 hour or until a wooden toothpick inserted near the center of the brownie portion comes out clean. Cool in pan on a wire rack at least 1 hour. Using foil, lift whole brownie from pan. Cut into 16 squares. Makes 16 brownies.

Nutrition information per brownie: 269 cal., 15 g total fat (7 g sat. fat), 63 mg chol., 107 mg sodium, 34 g carbo., 4 g pro.

Triple Peanut Bars

A drizzle of Peanut Butter Icing dresses up these bars for special occasions, but they taste every bit as scrumptious without it.

Nonstick cooking spray
1 18-ounce roll refrigerated peanut butter cookie dough
1 12-ounce package (2 cups) semisweet chocolate pieces
1 14-ounce can (1¼ cups) sweetened condensed milk
1½ cups dry-roasted peanuts
1 10-ounce package peanut butter-flavored pieces
Peanut Butter Icing (optional)

Lightly coat a 15×10×1-inch baking pan with cooking spray; set aside. Using floured hands, press cookie dough onto bottom of prepared pan.

Sprinkle chocolate pieces evenly over dough. Drizzle with sweetened condensed milk. Sprinkle with the peanuts and peanut butter pieces; press firmly.

Bake in a 350° oven about 25 minutes or until edges are firm. Cool in pan on a wire rack. If desired, drizzle with Peanut Butter Icing. Cut into bars. Store, covered, in the refrigerator. Makes about 72 bars.

Peanut Butter Icing: In a small bowl beat together 1 cup sifted powdered sugar, ¼ cup peanut butter, and 1 tablespoon milk. Beat in enough additional milk, 1 teaspoon at a time, to make an icing of drizzling consistency.

Nutrition information per bar: 111 cal., 6 g total fat (2 g sat. fat), 4 mg chol., 70 mg sodium, 11 g carbo., 2 g pro.

Cranberry-Macadamia Bars

Bake up a batch of these bars during the holiday/cranberry season. Like tiny slices of tart, they add a unique shape and bold color to your holiday cookie tray.

1¼ cups all-purpose flour
¾ cup sugar
½ cup butter
½ cup finely chopped macadamia nuts, hazelnuts (filberts), or pecans
2 beaten eggs
1¼ cups sugar
2 tablespoons milk
1 teaspoon finely shredded orange peel
1 teaspoon vanilla
1 cup finely chopped cranberries
½ cup finely chopped macadamia nuts, hazelnuts (filberts), or pecans
½ cup coconut

For crust, in a medium bowl stir together flour and the ¾ cup sugar. Using a pastry blender, cut in butter until mixture resembles coarse crumbs. Stir in ½ cup nuts. Press the mixture into the bottom of an ungreased 13×9×2-inch baking pan. Bake in a 350° oven for 10 to 15 minutes or until crust is light brown around edges.

Meanwhile, in a small bowl combine eggs, the 1¼ cups sugar, the milk, orange peel, and vanilla. Beat until combined. Pour over the hot crust. Sprinkle with cranberries, ½ cup nuts, and the coconut.

Bake about 30 minutes or until golden brown. Cool slightly in pan on a wire rack. While warm, cut into 24 bars; cut bars in half diagonally. Cool in pan. Makes 48 bars.

Nutrition information per bar: 88 cal., 4 g total fat (2 g sat. fat), 14 mg chol., 23 mg sodium, 12 g carbo., 1 g pro.

Fairy Drops

These cookies literally sparkle when spread with Almond Frosting and sprinkled with crushed candies. Or top them with a simple sprinkling of plain or colored sugar.

1   cup butter
1   cup sifted powdered sugar
1   cup granulated sugar
1   teaspoon baking soda
1   teaspoon cream of tartar
1   teaspoon salt
1   cup cooking oil
2   eggs
2   teaspoons almond extract
4½ cups all-purpose flour
    Plain or colored granulated sugar
      or Almond Frosting
    Crushed hard candies (optional)

In a large mixing bowl beat butter with an electric mixer on medium to high speed for 30 seconds. Add powdered sugar, the 1 cup granulated sugar, the baking soda, cream of tartar, and salt; beat until fluffy. Beat in oil, eggs, and almond extract just until combined.

Beat in as much of the flour as you can with the mixer. Stir in any remaining flour with a wooden spoon. Cover and chill the dough for 30 minutes.

Working with one-fourth of the dough at a time, shape dough into 1¼-inch balls. (The dough will be soft; keep it chilled as you work with a portion.) Arrange balls about 2 inches apart on an ungreased cookie sheet. With the palm of your hand or, if desired, the bottom of a glass or a patterned cookie stamp dipped in granulated sugar, gently flatten balls to about ¼-inch thickness. Sprinkle with plain or colored granulated sugar (unless flattened with sugared glass or stamp) or leave plain for frosting.

Bake in a 350° oven for 10 to 12 minutes or until edges just begin to brown. Transfer cookies to a wire rack; cool. If desired, frost the cookies with Almond Frosting and sprinkle with crushed candies. Makes about 84 cookies.

Almond Frosting: In a medium mixing bowl beat ½ cup butter with an electric mixer on medium to high speed until fluffy. Beat in ½ teaspoon almond extract and ½ teaspoon vanilla. Alternately add 2½ to 3½ cups sifted powdered sugar and 3 tablespoons half-and-half, light cream, or milk, beating until the frosting is smooth and of spreading consistency. If desired, stir in a few drops food coloring to tint frosting.

Nutrition information per cookie: 77 cal., 5 g total fat (2 g sat. fat), 10 mg chol., 61 mg sodium, 8 g carbo., 1 g pro.

Spiral Cookies

Make the dough for these whimsical pink-and-white spirals and chill it overnight. When company comes, just slice and bake them while you're making tea. You'll have pretty cookies to serve warm from the oven.

1   **cup butter**
1½ **cups sugar**
1½ **teaspoons baking powder**
½   **teaspoon salt**
1   **egg**
1   **teaspoon vanilla**
½   **teaspoon peppermint extract**
    (optional)
2½ **cups all-purpose flour**
    Red paste food coloring

In a large mixing bowl beat butter with an electric mixer on medium to high speed for 30 seconds. Add sugar, baking powder, and salt; beat until combined. Beat in the egg, vanilla, and, if desired, peppermint extract until combined. Beat in as much of the flour as you can with the mixer. Stir in any remaining flour with a wooden spoon.

Divide dough in half. Tint one portion of the dough with paste food coloring. Knead coloring into dough until well mixed. If dough is too sticky to handle, wrap each half in waxed paper or plastic wrap and chill about 1 hour or until easy to handle.

On a lightly floured surface, roll each half of dough into a 12×8-inch rectangle. Using a large spatula and your hands, place one rectangle on top of the other. Press down gently with your hands to seal. Starting from a long side, tightly roll up into a spiral. Wrap in waxed paper or plastic wrap and chill at least 2 hours or until firm.

Using a sharp knife, cut roll into ¼-inch slices. Place slices about 1 inch apart on an ungreased cookie sheet. Bake in a 375° oven for 8 to 10 minutes or until edges are firm and light brown.

Cool on cookie sheet for 1 minute. Transfer cookies to a wire rack; cool. Makes about 48 cookies.

Nutrition information per cookie: *81 cal., 4 g total fat (2 g sat. fat), 15 mg chol., 63 mg sodium, 11 g carbo., 1 g pro.*

Caraway Cookies

Popular in New England bakeries about a century ago, these crisp treats inspired homemakers to duplicate them at home. You'll be delightfully surprised by the burst of caraway in every sweet bite.

2 cups all-purpose flour
1 tablespoon caraway seeds
1 teaspoon baking powder
¼ teaspoon baking soda
¼ teaspoon salt
½ cup butter
1 cup sugar
2 eggs

In a medium bowl stir together flour, caraway seeds, baking powder, baking soda, and salt; set aside.

In a large mixing bowl beat butter with an electric mixer on medium to high speed for 30 seconds. Add sugar; beat until combined. Beat in eggs, one at a time, beating well after each addition. Beat in as much of the flour mixture as you can with the mixer. Stir in any remaining flour mixture with a wooden spoon. Divide dough in half. Cover and chill about 3 hours or until easy to handle.

Lightly grease a cookie sheet; set aside. On a lightly floured surface, roll each half of the dough to ⅛-inch thickness. Using 2½-inch cookie cutters, cut dough into desired shapes. Place cookies about 2 inches apart on the prepared cookie sheet.

Bake in a 375° oven for 7 to 8 minutes or until edges are light brown. Transfer the cookies to a wire rack; cool. Makes about 54 cookies.

Nutrition information per cookie: 48 cal., 2 g total fat (1 g sat. fat), 13 mg chol., 45 mg sodium, 7 g carbo., 1 g pro.

Nutmeg Cake with Lemon Sauce

This light spice cake fills the role of lunch-box treat or after-school snack.

  2 cups all-purpose flour
  1 teaspoon baking powder
  1 teaspoon baking soda
  1 teaspoon ground nutmeg
  ¼ teaspoon salt
  ¼ cup butter
  ¼ cup shortening
1½ cups sugar
  ½ teaspoon vanilla
  3 eggs
  1 cup buttermilk or sour milk*
      Lemon Sauce
      Lemon slices, halved (optional)

Grease a 13×9×2-inch baking pan; set aside. Combine flour, baking powder, baking soda, nutmeg, and salt; set aside.

In a large mixing bowl beat butter and shortening with an electric mixer on medium to high speed for 30 seconds. Add sugar and vanilla; beat until combined. Add eggs, one at a time, beating well after each addition. Alternately add flour mixture and buttermilk or sour milk, beating on low speed after each addition just until combined. Pour batter into prepared pan.

Bake in a 350° oven for 30 to 35 minutes or until a wooden toothpick inserted near center comes out clean. Cool cake slightly in pan on a wire rack. Serve the warm cake with Lemon Sauce. If desired, garnish with lemon slices. Makes 12 servings.

Lemon Sauce: In a small saucepan stir together ¾ cup sugar, 5 teaspoons cornstarch, and dash salt. Stir in 1 cup water. Cook and stir over medium heat until thickened and bubbly. Cook and stir for 2 minutes more. Remove from heat. Stir in 1 teaspoon finely shredded lemon peel, 3 tablespoons lemon juice, 2 tablespoons butter, and, if desired, 1 drop yellow food coloring.

*Note: To make sour milk, place 1 tablespoon lemon juice or vinegar in a glass measuring cup. Add enough milk to make 1 cup total liquid; stir. Let stand for 5 minutes before using.

Nutrition information per serving: 338 cal., 12 g total fat (5 g sat. fat), 69 mg chol., 297 mg sodium, 55 g carbo., 4 g pro.

Granny Cake

Also known as the "hummingbird cake," this homey, church-social-style recipe has been shared over backyard fences for years.

3 cups all-purpose flour
2 cups granulated sugar
1 teaspoon baking soda
1 teaspoon ground nutmeg
½ teaspoon salt
½ teaspoon ground cloves
¾ cup butter
2 cups mashed ripe bananas
1 8-ounce can crushed pineapple
3 eggs
2 teaspoons vanilla
1 cup finely chopped pecans
   Powdered sugar (optional)

Grease and flour a 10-inch fluted tube pan; set aside. In a medium bowl stir together flour, granulated sugar, baking soda, nutmeg, salt, and cloves; set aside.

In a large mixing bowl beat butter with an electric mixer on medium to high speed for 30 seconds. Add bananas, undrained pineapple, eggs, and vanilla; beat until combined. Add flour mixture. Beat on low speed until combined. Beat on medium speed for 1 minute. Fold in pecans. Spread batter in the prepared pan.

Bake in a 325° oven for 70 to 75 minutes or until a wooden toothpick inserted near center comes out clean. Cool in pan on a wire rack for 10 minutes. Remove from pan. Cool completely on wire rack.

If desired, decorate cake with a powdered-sugar design. Place a paper doily on top of cake. Sift powdered sugar over doily to fill cutout designs. Carefully remove doily. Makes 12 servings.

Nutrition information per serving: 481 cal., 19 g total fat (8 g sat. fat), 84 mg chol., 328 mg sodium, 74 g carbo., 6 g pro.

Upside-Down Chip Cake

Carefully spoon the cake batter over the coconut and pecans so, when the cake is inverted, the topping stays evenly distributed.

3 tablespoons butter
½ cup packed brown sugar
4 teaspoons water
½ cup coconut
½ cup coarsely chopped pecans
1 cup all-purpose flour
⅔ cup granulated sugar
½ cup unsweetened cocoa powder
¼ cup packed brown sugar
2 teaspoons baking powder
½ cup milk
¼ cup butter, softened
2 eggs
1 teaspoon vanilla
¾ cup miniature semisweet
     chocolate pieces

Place the 3 tablespoons butter in a 9×1½-inch round baking pan. Heat in a 350° oven until butter is melted. Stir in the ½ cup brown sugar and the water. Sprinkle with coconut and pecans. Set aside.

In a medium mixing bowl stir together flour, granulated sugar, cocoa powder, the ¼ cup brown sugar, and the baking powder. Add milk, the ¼ cup butter, the eggs, and vanilla.

Beat with an electric mixer on low speed until combined. Beat on medium speed for 1 minute. By hand, stir in ½ cup of the chocolate pieces. Spoon batter into the prepared pan.

Bake for 40 to 45 minutes or until cake feels firm in center when lightly touched. Cool in pan on a wire rack for 5 minutes. Loosen edge of cake from pan; invert onto a serving plate.

Immediately sprinkle remaining chocolate pieces over topping. Let stand about 30 minutes before slicing. Serve warm. Makes 8 servings.

Nutrition information per serving: 456 cal., 24 g total fat (11 g sat. fat), 83 mg chol., 239 mg sodium, 52 g carbo., 6 g pro.

Tiramisu

This recipe simplifies classic tiramisu (tee-rah-MEE-su) by using a purchased angel cake. Most important, it's as light as a feather.

1   8-ounce package reduced-fat cream
    cheese (Neufchâtel), softened
½   cup sifted powdered sugar
3   tablespoons coffee liqueur
1   8-ounce container frozen light
    whipped dessert topping, thawed
¼   cup fat-free dairy sour cream
2   tablespoons coffee liqueur
1   8- to 10-inch round angel food cake
¼   cup strong black coffee
2   tablespoons coffee liqueur
    Mocha Fudge Sauce (optional)
    Edible flowers (optional)

For filling, in a large mixing bowl combine the cream cheese, powdered sugar, and the 3 tablespoons coffee liqueur. Beat with an electric mixer on medium speed until blended and smooth. Stir in ½ cup of the whipped dessert topping. Set aside.

For frosting, in a medium bowl combine remaining whipped dessert topping, the sour cream, and 2 tablespoons coffee liqueur. Set aside.

Using a serrated knife, cut the angel food cake horizontally into three layers. Place one layer on a serving platter and two layers on large dinner plates. Using a long-tined fork or a skewer, poke holes in tops of all three layers. In a small bowl combine the coffee and 2 tablespoons coffee liqueur; drizzle over all layers. Spread the first layer with half of the filling. Add a second layer and spread with the remaining filling. Add top layer of cake. Frost cake with the frosting. (If desired, cover and chill up to 4 hours.)

If desired, just before serving, drizzle top and sides with some of the Mocha Fudge Sauce. If using, drizzle dessert plates with the remaining sauce; cut cake into wedges and place wedges on top of sauce. If desired, garnish with flowers. Makes 16 servings.

Mocha Fudge Sauce: In a small bowl dissolve 1 teaspoon instant coffee crystals in 1 teaspoon hot water. Stir in ¼ cup chocolate-flavored syrup.

Nutrition information per serving: 155 cal., 5 g total fat (4 g sat. fat), 11 mg chol., 203 mg sodium, 21 g carbo., 3 g pro.

Carrot Cake with Lemony Icing

This show-off makes its mark with sweet spring carrots and buttermilk cake batter. As if that's not enough, it's topped off with chunky walnuts and thick lemon icing.

2	cups all-purpose flour
1	teaspoon baking powder
½	teaspoon baking soda
⅛	teaspoon salt
½	cup shortening
1¾	cups sugar
1	teaspoon vanilla
4	egg whites
1	cup buttermilk or sour milk (see note, page 238)
2½	cups shredded carrots
	Lemony Icing
1	cup chopped walnuts
	Walnut halves (optional)
	Carrot curls (optional)

Grease and lightly flour two 8×1½-inch or 9×1½-inch round baking pans; set aside. Stir together flour, baking powder, baking soda, and salt; set aside.

In a large mixing bowl beat shortening with an electric mixer on medium to high speed for 30 seconds. Add sugar and vanilla; beat until combined. Add egg whites, one at a time, beating well after each addition. Alternately add flour mixture and buttermilk or sour milk, beating on low speed after each addition just until combined. Using a wooden spoon, stir in shredded carrots. Divide batter between the prepared pans.

Bake in a 350° oven for 35 to 40 minutes for 8-inch pans (30 to 35 minutes for 9-inch pans) or until a wooden toothpick inserted near centers comes out clean. Cool in pans on wire racks for 10 minutes. Remove from pans. Cool completely on wire racks. Prepare the Lemony Icing.

To assemble cake, place one cake layer on a serving plate. Spoon about ⅔ cup icing over top of layer. Sprinkle with half of the chopped walnuts. Place the second cake layer, top side up, on first layer. Spoon the remaining icing over top of cake. Sprinkle with the remaining chopped walnuts. If desired, garnish with walnut halves and carrot curls. Makes 12 servings.

Lemony Icing: In a medium bowl stir together 3 cups sifted powdered sugar and enough lemon juice (about 3 tablespoons) to make an icing of glazing consistency.

Nutrition information per serving: 444 cal., 15 g total fat (3 g sat. fat), 1 mg chol., 160 mg sodium, 73 g carbo., 6 g pro.

Deep Chocolate Cake with Malt Topping

It's hip to be square, but this stunning cake can be round too. Use 9×1½-inch round baking pans instead of 8-inch square pans.

½ cup unsweetened cocoa powder
2 cups all-purpose flour
1 teaspoon baking powder
½ teaspoon baking soda
⅔ cup butter
1¾ cups sugar
3 eggs
4 ounces unsweetened chocolate,
    melted and cooled
2 teaspoons vanilla
1½ cups milk
    Chocolate Malt Frosting
2 cups malted milk balls or miniature
    malted milk balls

Grease three 8×8×2-inch baking pans; lightly dust each pan with 1 teaspoon of the cocoa powder. Set aside. In a medium bowl stir together flour, baking powder, baking soda, and the remaining cocoa powder. Set aside.

In a large mixing bowl beat butter with an electric mixer on medium to high speed for 30 seconds. Add sugar; beat until combined. Add eggs, one at a time, beating well after each addition. Beat in chocolate and vanilla. Alternately add flour mixture and milk, beating on low speed after each addition until combined. Divide among prepared pans.

Bake in a 350° oven for 17 to 20 minutes or until a wooden toothpick inserted near the centers comes out clean. Cool in pans on wire racks for 10 minutes. Remove from pans. Cool completely on wire racks. Prepare the Chocolate Malt Frosting.

To assemble cake, spread ¾ cup of the frosting on the tops of 2 of the cake layers; stack layers. Add top layer; frost the top and sides of the cake, reserving some frosting for piping. Place the remaining frosting in a decorating bag fitted with a medium round tip. Starting from the bottom, pipe a zigzag pattern on sides and top edge of cake. If desired, coarsely chop or halve some of the malted milk balls. Decorate the cake with milk balls. Store, covered, in the refrigerator. Makes 20 servings.

Chocolate Malt Frosting: In a large saucepan bring 2 cups whipping cream just to boiling over medium-high heat. Remove from heat. Stir in ⅓ cup malt powder. Add two 11½-ounce packages milk chocolate pieces (do not stir). Cover and let stand for 5 minutes. Stir until smooth. Transfer to a large mixing bowl (mixture will be thin). Cover and chill for 3 hours. Set bowl of frosting in a larger bowl of ice water. Beat frosting with an electric mixer on medium speed about 3 minutes or until fluffy and of spreading consistency.

Nutrition information per serving: 540 cal., 32 g total fat (17 g sat. fat), 83 mg chol., 263 mg sodium, 61 g carbo., 8 g pro.

Daffodil Cake

Celebrate the rites of spring with this classic angel food cake marbled with lemon-yellow sponge cake. It's only fitting that your table feature a simple centerpiece with daffodils from your garden.

1½ cups egg whites (11 or 12 large)
 1 cup sifted cake flour or sifted
    all-purpose flour
 ¾ cup granulated sugar
 2 teaspoons vanilla
1½ teaspoons cream of tartar
 ¼ teaspoon salt
 ¾ cup granulated sugar
 6 egg yolks
1½ teaspoons finely shredded
    lemon peel
    Tangy Lemon Frosting
    Finely shredded lemon peel
    (optional)

In a very large mixing bowl allow egg whites to stand at room temperature for 30 minutes. Meanwhile, sift together flour and ¾ cup granulated sugar three times. Set aside. Add vanilla, cream of tartar, and salt to egg whites. Beat with an electric mixer on medium to high speed until soft peaks form (tips curl). Gradually add ¾ cup granulated sugar, about 2 tablespoons at a time, beating until stiff peaks form (tips stand straight). Sift one-fourth of the flour mixture over egg white mixture; fold in gently. (If too full, transfer to a larger bowl.) Repeat with the remaining flour mixture, using one-fourth of the mixture each time. Transfer half of the batter to another bowl.

In a small mixing bowl beat egg yolks on high speed about 6 minutes or until thick and lemon colored. Fold in the 1½ teaspoons lemon peel. Gently fold yolk mixture into half of the batter. Alternately spoon yellow batter and white batter into an ungreased 10-inch tube pan. Swirl a metal spatula through batters to marble.

Bake on the lowest rack in a 350° oven for 40 to 45 minutes or until top springs back when lightly touched. Immediately invert cake in pan; cool completely. Remove from pan. Place upside down on a serving plate. Frost with Tangy Lemon Frosting. If desired, sprinkle with additional lemon peel. Makes 12 servings.

Tangy Lemon Frosting: In a large mixing bowl beat ½ cup butter with an electric mixer on medium to high speed for 30 seconds. Gradually beat in 5½ cups sifted powdered sugar, ½ teaspoon finely shredded lemon peel, and ⅓ cup lemon juice. Beat in enough additional lemon juice, if necessary, to make a frosting of spreading consistency.

Nutrition information per serving: 424 cal., 10 g total fat (5 g sat. fat), 127 mg chol., 189 mg sodium, 79 g carbo., 5 g pro.

Amazing Banana Nut Roll

Some jelly-roll cakes require rolling twice. Not this one! The layers bake together, creating a wonderful banana cake and cream cheese filling, which is easily rolled into one memorable dessert.

½ cup all-purpose flour
½ teaspoon baking powder
¼ teaspoon baking soda
1 8-ounce package cream cheese, softened
1 3-ounce package cream cheese, softened
½ cup granulated sugar
1 egg
3 tablespoons milk
4 egg yolks
½ teaspoon vanilla
⅓ cup granulated sugar
1 large banana, mashed (about ½ cup)
½ cup finely chopped walnuts or pecans
4 egg whites
½ cup granulated sugar
   Sifted powdered sugar
   Vanilla Cream Cheese Frosting
   Chocolate-flavored syrup (optional)

Lightly grease a 15×10×1-inch baking pan. Line bottom with waxed paper; grease paper. Set pan aside. In a small bowl stir together flour, baking powder, and baking soda. Set aside.

For filling, in a medium mixing bowl combine cream cheese and the ½ cup granulated sugar. Beat with an electric mixer on medium speed until smooth. Add whole egg and milk; beat until combined. Spread in the prepared pan; set aside. In another medium mixing bowl beat egg yolks and vanilla on medium speed about 5 minutes or until thick and lemon colored. Gradually add the ⅓ cup granulated sugar, beating until sugar is dissolved. Stir in banana and nuts.

Thoroughly wash beaters. In a large mixing bowl beat egg whites on medium speed until soft peaks form (tips curl). Gradually add the ½ cup granulated sugar, beating on high speed until stiff peaks form (tips stand straight). Fold yolk mixture into egg whites. Sprinkle the flour mixture evenly over egg mixture; fold in just until combined. Carefully spread over filling in pan. Bake in a 375° oven for 15 to 20 minutes or until top springs back when lightly touched.

Immediately loosen edges of cake from pan and turn cake out onto a towel sprinkled with powdered sugar. Carefully peel off paper. Starting from a short side, roll up cake into a spiral, using the towel as a guide but not rolling towel into cake. Cool on a wire rack. Spread top with Vanilla Cream Cheese Frosting. If desired, drizzle with chocolate syrup. Makes 10 servings.

Vanilla Cream Cheese Frosting: In a mixing bowl combine one-half of a 3-ounce package cream cheese, softened, and ½ teaspoon vanilla. Beat with an electric mixer on medium speed until light and fluffy. Gradually beat in 1 cup sifted powdered sugar. Beat in enough milk (1 to 2 tablespoons) to make a frosting of spreading consistency.

Nutrition information per serving: 400 cal., 19 g total fat (9 g sat. fat), 146 mg chol., 162 mg sodium, 51 g carbo., 8 g pro.

Desserts

Contents

FRESH PEAR CUSTARD TART
(recipe, page 266)

For more recipes, visit our Recipe Center at www.bhg.com/bkrecipe

Blueberries with Shortcake Drops

The tiny shortcakes make a great solo snack, and they're even yummier buried in a little bowl of blueberries and berry syrup.

1½ cups all-purpose flour
2 tablespoons sugar
1 teaspoon baking powder
¼ teaspoon baking soda
¼ teaspoon ground cardamom
   (optional)
⅓ cup cold butter
1 beaten egg
¼ cup plain low-fat yogurt
3 tablespoons milk
4 cups blueberries
   Blueberry-Cardamom Syrup

Grease a baking sheet; set aside. For shortcake drops, in a medium bowl stir together flour, the 2 tablespoons sugar, the baking powder, baking soda, and, if desired, cardamom. Using a pastry blender, cut in butter until mixture resembles coarse crumbs.

In a small bowl combine egg, yogurt, and milk. Add to flour mixture, stirring just until moistened. Drop dough by a teaspoon into 1-inch mounds onto the prepared baking sheet.

Bake in a 400° oven about 10 minutes or until golden brown. Transfer shortcake drops to a wire rack; cool slightly.

Divide shortcake drops and blueberries among dessert dishes. Drizzle with Blueberry-Cardamom Syrup. Makes 6 servings.

Blueberry-Cardamom Syrup: In a small saucepan combine 1 cup blueberries, ½ cup water, ¼ cup sugar, 2 teaspoons lime juice or lemon juice, and ¼ teaspoon ground cardamom. Bring to boiling, stirring to dissolve sugar; reduce heat. Simmer, uncovered, about 10 minutes or until slightly thickened, stirring occasionally. Remove from heat; cool slightly. Pour the syrup through a fine-mesh sieve; discard solids. Cool. Makes ¾ cup.

Nutrition information per serving: 382 cal., 12 g total fat (7 g sat. fat), 66 mg chol., 259 mg sodium, 64 g carbo., 6 g pro.

Peach and Almond Crisp

Select peaches that have a healthy golden yellow skin without tinges of green. Ripe fruit yields slightly to gentle pressure.

8	cups sliced, peeled peaches or nectarines or frozen unsweetened peach slices
⅔	cup packed brown sugar
¾	cup all-purpose flour
½	cup rolled oats
½	cup sliced almonds, toasted
3	tablespoons granulated sugar
½	cup butter
⅓	cup granulated sugar
½	teaspoon ground cinnamon
¼	teaspoon ground nutmeg
⅛	teaspoon ground ginger
¼	cup peach nectar or orange juice
	Vanilla ice cream (optional)

Thaw peaches, if frozen. Do not drain. For topping, in a medium bowl stir together brown sugar, ½ cup of the flour, the oats, almonds, and the 3 tablespoons granulated sugar. Using a pastry blender, cut in butter until mixture resembles coarse crumbs.

For filling, in a large bowl stir together the remaining flour, the ⅓ cup granulated sugar, the cinnamon, nutmeg, and ginger. Add the peach or nectarine slices with their juice and peach nectar or orange juice; toss gently to coat. Transfer filling to an ungreased 3-quart rectangular baking dish. Sprinkle with topping.

Bake in a 400° oven for 30 to 35 minutes or until fruit is tender and topping is golden brown. Serve warm or at room temperature. If desired, serve with ice cream. Makes 12 servings.

Nutrition information per serving: 258 cal., 11 g total fat (5 g sat. fat), 20 mg chol., 94 mg sodium, 40 g carbo., 3 g pro.

ℙEACH POINTERS

To ripen peaches, place them in a paper bag at room temperature for a few days or until desired ripeness. Once the peaches are ripe, store them in the refrigerator. To remove the peel from a peach, dip the peach into boiling water for 20 seconds. Then use a paring knife to remove the skin. If the skin doesn't peel easily, return the peach to the boiling water for a few more seconds.

Chocolate-Sauced Pears

Say yes to dessert. These luscious pears contain fewer than than 120 calories and only 1 gram of fat per serving.

4   small pears
2   tablespoons lemon juice
2   teaspoons vanilla
½   teaspoon ground cinnamon
2   tablespoons chocolate-flavored syrup

Core pears from bottom ends, leaving stems intact. Peel pears. If necessary, cut a thin slice from bottoms of pears to help them stand upright. Place pears in a 2-quart square baking dish. In a small bowl stir together lemon juice, vanilla, and cinnamon; brush onto pears. Pour any extra lemon juice mixture over pears.

Cover and bake in a 375° oven for 30 to 35 minutes or until pears are tender. Cool slightly.

To serve, place warm pears, stem ends up, in dessert dishes. Pour the baking liquid through a fine-mesh sieve placed over a small bowl; discard solids. Stir chocolate syrup into strained liquid; drizzle over pears. Makes 4 servings.

Nutrition information per serving: 116 cal., 1 g total fat (0 g sat. fat), 0 mg chol., 5 mg sodium, 29 g carbo., 1 g pro.

Maple-Glazed Bananas

Warm and buttery maple sauce flavors every scrumptious bite of this rich dessert.

½   cup butter or margarine
½   cup packed brown sugar
½   cup pure maple syrup or maple-flavored syrup
1   teaspoon finely shredded lemon peel
1   tablespoon lemon juice
¼   teaspoon ground cloves
6   firm, ripe bananas, halved lengthwise and cut into 1-inch pieces
1   quart vanilla ice cream

In a heavy large skillet melt butter or margarine over medium heat. Stir in brown sugar, maple syrup, lemon peel, lemon juice, and cloves. Bring to boiling; reduce heat. Simmer, uncovered, for 2 minutes.

Add bananas; spoon some of the syrup mixture over bananas. Cover and cook about 2 minutes more or until heated through.

Scoop ice cream into dessert dishes. Spoon the warm bananas and syrup mixture over ice cream. Makes 8 servings.

Nutrition information per serving: 403 cal., 19 g total fat (12 g sat. fat), 60 mg chol., 175 mg sodium, 60 g carbo., 3 g pro.

Chocolate-Sauced Pears

Pineapple-Orange Crepes

If you like, make the crepes up to two days before serving them. Stack them with waxed paper between the layers and store in an airtight container in the refrigerator.

½ cup all-purpose flour
⅓ cup milk
½ teaspoon finely shredded orange peel
⅓ cup orange juice
1 egg
2 teaspoons cooking oil
½ of a fresh pineapple, peeled, cored, and sliced
2 tablespoons butter or margarine
¼ cup packed brown sugar
1 tablespoon cornstarch
½ cup orange juice
2 medium oranges, peeled and sectioned
1 tablespoon rum (optional)
¼ cup chopped pecans or slivered almonds, toasted
¼ cup coconut, toasted
   Strawberries (optional)

For crepes, in a small bowl combine the flour, milk, orange peel, the ⅓ cup orange juice, the egg, and oil. Beat with a rotary beater until well mixed.

Heat a lightly greased 6-inch skillet over medium heat. Spoon 2 tablespoons of the batter into the skillet; lift and tilt the skillet to spread batter. Return to heat; brown on one side only. Invert pan over paper towels; remove crepe. Repeat with the remaining batter, greasing skillet occasionally.

Fold each crepe in half, browned side out. Fold in half again, forming a triangle. Place crepes in a single layer on a baking sheet. Keep warm in a 300° oven while making the sauce.

For sauce, cut the pineapple slices into fourths; set aside. In a medium saucepan melt butter or margarine. Stir in brown sugar and cornstarch. Add the ½ cup orange juice. Cook and stir until thickened and bubbly. Cook and stir for 1 minute more. Add the pineapple, orange sections, and, if desired, rum. Cook over low heat, stirring gently, until heated through.

Arrange folded crepes on dessert plates. Spoon the sauce over crepes. Sprinkle with toasted nuts and coconut. If desired, garnish with strawberries. Makes 4 servings.

Nutrition information per serving: 345 cal., 17 g total fat (5 g sat. fat), 70 mg chol., 102 mg sodium, 45 g carbo., 6 g pro.

Double Raspberry Cheesecake

This raspberry-studded, ricotta cheesecake topped with a glistening red raspberry sauce is anything but ordinary.

1½ cups finely crushed graham crackers
¼ cup butter or margarine, melted
2 8-ounce packages cream cheese, softened
1 cup ricotta cheese
1¼ cups sugar
3 tablespoons all-purpose flour
1 teaspoon lemon extract
3 slightly beaten eggs
⅔ cup raspberries
   Raspberry Sauce

For crust, in a small bowl combine crushed graham crackers and melted butter or margarine. Press mixture firmly into the bottom and about 1½ inches up the side of a 9-inch springform pan. Set aside.

In a large mixing bowl combine cream cheese, ricotta cheese, sugar, flour, and lemon extract. Beat with an electric mixer on low speed until combined. Add eggs all at once and beat on low speed just until combined. Gently fold in raspberries. Pour batter into prepared pan.

Bake in a 375° oven for 35 to 40 minutes or until center appears nearly set when shaken. Cool in pan on a wire rack for 15 minutes. Loosen crust from side of pan; cool for 30 minutes more. Remove side of pan. Cover and chill for 4 to 24 hours. Serve with Raspberry Sauce. Makes 12 servings.

Raspberry Sauce: In a medium saucepan stir together 1 cup raspberry-cranberry juice and 1 tablespoon cornstarch. Cook and stir until thickened and bubbly. Add ¼ cup currant jelly, stirring until melted. Remove from heat. Stir in 1 cup fresh or frozen red raspberries, thawed, and, if desired, 1 tablespoon crème de cassis. Cover and chill until serving time.

Nutrition information per serving: 390 cal., 21 g total fat (12 g sat. fat), 112 mg chol., 254 mg sodium, 43 g carbo., 8 g pro.

Coffee Éclairs

These sumptuous, tender shells are filled with ice cream and topped with a smooth coffee-flavored sauce.

1	cup water
½	cup butter
1	cup all-purpose flour
4	eggs
1	quart coffee or vanilla ice cream
1½	cups cold water
3	tablespoons cornstarch
1	tablespoon instant coffee crystals
1	cup light-colored corn syrup
2	tablespoons butter
1	teaspoon vanilla
½	cup chopped pecans (optional)

Grease a large baking sheet; set aside. In a medium saucepan combine the 1 cup water and the ½ cup butter. Bring to boiling. Add flour all at once, stirring vigorously. Cook and stir until mixture forms a ball that doesn't separate. Remove from heat. Cool for 10 minutes. Add eggs, one at a time, beating well after each addition until smooth.

Spoon dough into a decorating bag fitted with a large plain round tip (about ½-inch opening). Pipe 10 to 12 strips of dough, about 3 inches apart, onto the prepared baking sheet, making each strip about 4 inches long, 1 inch wide, and ¾ inch high.

Bake in a 400° oven about 40 minutes or until golden brown. Transfer to a wire rack; cool. Cut éclairs in half lengthwise and remove soft dough from centers. Fill bottom halves with ice cream; replace tops. Cover and freeze until serving time.

Meanwhile, for sauce, in a medium saucepan combine the 1½ cups cold water, the cornstarch, and coffee crystals. Stir in corn syrup. Cook and stir until thickened and bubbly. Cook and stir for 2 minutes more. Remove from heat. Add the 2 tablespoons butter and the vanilla; stir until butter is melted.

To serve, remove éclairs from freezer and let stand about 15 minutes to soften. Spoon some of the warm sauce over éclairs. If desired, sprinkle with pecans. (Cover and chill any leftover sauce up to 1 week. Reheat sauce and serve with ice cream.) Makes 10 to 12 éclairs.

Nutrition information per éclair: 385 cal., 19 g total fat (11 g sat. fat), 139 mg chol., 207 mg sodium, 49 g carbo., 6 g pro.

Fresh Pear Custard Tart

Be sure to use ripe pears for this tart. Those that are too firm or unripe make it difficult to eat. If you're really in a pinch, substitute sliced, well-drained canned pears.

Baked Tart Shell
½ cup granulated sugar
2 tablespoons cornstarch
2 cups fat-free milk
2 beaten eggs
4 teaspoons finely chopped crystallized ginger
1 teaspoon vanilla
⅔ cup pear nectar
1½ teaspoons cornstarch
3 ripe small pears
½ cup berries (such as raspberries, blackberries, and/or blueberries)
Desired garnishes (such as sifted powdered sugar, mint leaves, and/or edible flowers)

Prepare Baked Tart Shell. For vanilla cream, in a heavy medium saucepan combine granulated sugar and the 2 tablespoons cornstarch. Stir in milk. Cook and stir over medium heat until thickened and bubbly. Cook and stir for 2 minutes more. Remove from heat.

Gradually stir about 1 cup of the hot mixture into beaten eggs. Return all of the egg mixture to saucepan. Stir in ginger. Cook and stir until bubbly; reduce heat. Cook and stir for 2 minutes more. Remove from heat. Stir in vanilla. Pour the vanilla cream into tart shell. Cover and chill until ready to assemble.

Meanwhile, for glaze, in a small saucepan combine pear nectar and the 1½ teaspoons cornstarch. Cook and stir until thickened and bubbly. Cook and stir for 2 minutes more. Remove from heat. Cover and cool to room temperature.

To assemble tart, peel, core, and thinly slice pears. Arrange pear slices in a concentric pattern over the vanilla cream. Pour the cooled glaze over pears, spreading evenly. Cover and chill for 1 to 4 hours. To serve, sprinkle the tart with berries. Top with desired garnishes. Makes 10 servings.

Baked Tart Shell: In a medium bowl stir together 1¼ cups all-purpose flour and ¼ teaspoon salt. Combine ¼ cup fat-free milk and 3 tablespoons cooking oil; add all at once to flour mixture. Stir with a fork until a dough forms. Form into a ball. On a lightly floured surface, roll dough from center to edge into a 13-inch circle. Ease pastry into an 11-inch tart pan with a removable bottom, being careful not to stretch pastry. Trim pastry even with rim of tart pan. Generously prick bottom, sides, and corners of pastry with a fork. Bake in a 450° oven for 10 to 12 minutes or until golden brown. Cool on a wire rack.

Nutrition information per serving: 216 cal., 6 g total fat (1 g sat. fat), 44 mg chol., 96 mg sodium, 37 g carbo., 5 g pro.

Chocolate-Topped Fruited Phyllo Tarts

Flaky phyllo pastry meets indulgent chocolate and sweet-tart dried fruit in these irresistible bite-size tarts. To make them ahead, store, covered, in the refrigerator up to two days. Before serving, let stand at room temperature about 30 minutes.

6	ounces semisweet chocolate, cut up
¼	cup whipping cream
¼	cup snipped dried apricots
¼	cup snipped dried cherries
¼	cup brandy
½	cup finely chopped almonds
24	1¾-inch baked miniature phyllo shells

In a medium saucepan combine chocolate and whipping cream. Cook and stir over low heat until smooth. Remove from heat; cool.

In a small bowl combine apricots, cherries, and brandy. Cover and let stand about 45 minutes or until fruit is softened; drain well. Stir in ¼ cup of the almonds.

Place about 1 teaspoon of the fruit mixture in the bottom of each phyllo shell. Spoon about 1 teaspoon of the chocolate mixture into each shell. Sprinkle with the remaining almonds. Makes 24 tarts.

Nutrition information per tart: *93 cal., 6 g total fat (2 g sat. fat), 4 mg chol., 11 mg sodium, 9 g carbo., 2 g pro.*

Apple-Cranberry Streusel Pie

A whisper of cream gives the filling of this streusel-crowned creation a touch of richness. Dried cranberries or tart cherries provide lively bursts of flavor.

Baked Pastry Shell
½ cup dried cranberries or dried tart cherries
6 large cooking apples, peeled, cored, and sliced (6 cups)
⅔ cup granulated sugar
3 tablespoons all-purpose flour
1 teaspoon apple pie spice
1 teaspoon finely shredded lemon peel
¼ teaspoon salt
⅓ cup half-and-half or light cream
⅓ cup all-purpose flour
⅓ cup packed brown sugar
⅓ cup finely chopped pecans or walnuts, toasted
¼ teaspoon ground nutmeg
3 tablespoons butter
Vanilla Icing

Prepare Baked Pastry Shell. Reduce the oven temperature to 375°. In a small bowl cover dried cranberries or cherries with boiling water. Cover and let stand for 5 minutes; drain.

For filling, in a large bowl combine apples and cranberries or cherries. Spoon filling into pastry shell. In a small bowl combine granulated sugar, the 3 tablespoons flour, the apple pie spice, lemon peel, and salt. Stir in half-and-half or light cream. Pour over filling. For topping, in a medium bowl combine the ⅓ cup flour, the brown sugar, nuts, and nutmeg. Using a pastry blender, cut in butter until the pieces are pea-size. Sprinkle over filling. To prevent overbrowning, cover edges of pie with foil.

Bake in the 375° oven for 45 minutes. Remove foil. Bake for 10 to 15 minutes more or until topping is golden brown and fruit is tender. Cool on a wire rack for 45 minutes. Drizzle with Vanilla Icing. Serve warm or cool. Store, covered, in the refrigerator. Makes 8 servings.

Baked Pastry Shell: In a medium bowl stir together 1¼ cups all-purpose flour and ¼ teaspoon salt. Using a pastry blender, cut in ⅓ cup shortening until pieces are pea-size. Using 4 to 5 tablespoons cold water, sprinkle 1 tablespoon water at a time over mixture, gently tossing with a fork until all is moistened. Form into a ball. On a lightly floured surface, roll from center to edge into a 12-inch circle. Ease pastry into a 9-inch pie plate, being careful not to stretch pastry. Trim ½ inch beyond edge. Fold under extra pastry; crimp edge. Line pastry with a double thickness of foil. Bake in a 450° oven for 8 minutes. Remove foil. Bake for 5 to 6 minutes more until golden brown. Cool.

Vanilla Icing: In a small bowl combine ½ cup sifted powdered sugar, 1 teaspoon milk, and ¼ teaspoon vanilla. Stir in enough additional milk, 1 teaspoon at a time, to make an icing of drizzling consistency.

Nutrition information per serving: 447 cal., 18 g total fat (9 g sat. fat), 15 mg chol., 186 mg sodium, 72 g carbo., 4 g pro.

Cheddar-Rosemary-Crusted Pear Pie

The sweetness of firm, ripe pears complements the assertive flavor of fresh rosemary found in the pastry. Cheddar cheese bonds the three flavors together.

Cheddar-Rosemary Pastry
¾ cup sugar
3 tablespoons cornstarch
2 tablespoons pear nectar, orange juice, or apple juice
8 cups thinly sliced, peeled pears
White cheddar cheese (optional)
Fresh rosemary sprigs (optional)

Prepare Cheddar-Rosemary Pastry. On a lightly floured surface, roll half of the dough from center to edge into a 13-inch circle. Ease pastry into a 9- or 9½-inch deep-dish pie plate, being careful not to stretch the pastry.

For filling, in a large bowl stir together sugar and cornstarch. Stir in nectar or fruit juice. Add pear slices; toss gently to coat. Spoon filling into pastry-lined pie plate. Trim pastry even with rim of pie plate.

Roll remaining dough into a 12-inch circle. Cut slits to allow steam to escape. Place pastry on filling; trim ½ inch beyond edge of pie plate. Fold top pastry under bottom pastry; crimp edge. To prevent overbrowning, cover edges of pie with foil. Place pie on a baking sheet.

Bake in a 375° oven for 25 minutes. Remove foil. Bake for 25 to 35 minutes more or until top is golden brown and filling is bubbly. Cool on a wire rack.

To serve, cut pie into wedges. If desired, serve with white cheddar cheese and garnish with rosemary sprigs. Makes 8 servings.

Cheddar-Rosemary Pastry: In a large bowl stir together 2½ cups all-purpose flour, 1½ teaspoons snipped fresh rosemary, and ½ teaspoon salt. Using a pastry blender, cut in ⅔ cup shortening until pieces are pea-size. Stir in ½ cup finely shredded white cheddar cheese (2 ounces). Using 7 to 8 tablespoons cold water, sprinkle 1 tablespoon water at a time over mixture, gently tossing with a fork until all is moistened. Divide in half. Form each half into a ball.

Nutrition information per serving: 496 cal., 19 g total fat (6 g sat. fat), 7 mg chol., 191 mg sodium, 76 g carbo., 6 g pro.

Mince-Peach Pie

Although traditionally made with minced meat and suet, you can purchase today's all-fruit mincemeat in jars.

Pastry for Double-Crust Pie
1 29-ounce can peach slices, drained and cut up
1 27-ounce jar (2⅔ cups) mincemeat
  Milk (optional)
  Granulated sugar (optional)
  Vanilla ice cream or Hard Sauce (optional)

Prepare Pastry for Double-Crust Pie. On a lightly floured surface, roll half of the dough from center to edge into a 12-inch circle. Ease pastry into a 9-inch pie plate, being careful not to stretch pastry.

For filling, in a large bowl stir together peaches and mincemeat. Spoon the filling into pastry-lined pie plate. Trim the pastry even with rim of pie plate.

Roll remaining dough into a 12-inch circle. Using hors d'oeuvre cutters, make cutouts in dough to allow steam to escape. Place pastry on filling; trim ½ inch beyond edge of pie plate. Fold top pastry under bottom pastry; crimp edge. If desired, brush pastry with milk and sprinkle with granulated sugar. To prevent overbrowning, cover edges of pie with foil. Place pie on a baking sheet.

Bake in a 375° oven for 25 minutes. Remove foil. Bake for 20 to 25 minutes more or until pastry is golden brown. Cool on a wire rack. To serve, cut pie into wedges. If desired, serve with ice cream or Hard Sauce. Makes 8 servings.

Pastry for Double-Crust Pie: In a large bowl stir together 2 cups all-purpose flour and ½ teaspoon salt. Using a pastry blender, cut in ⅔ cup shortening until pieces are pea-size. Using 6 to 7 tablespoons cold water, sprinkle 1 tablespoon water at a time over mixture, gently tossing with a fork until all is moistened. Divide dough in half. Form each half into a ball.

Hard Sauce: In a small bowl beat together 1¼ cups sifted powdered sugar and ¾ cup softened butter until fluffy. Beat in 3 tablespoons brandy, rum, or orange juice and ½ teaspoon vanilla. Store, covered, in the refrigerator up to 2 weeks. Let stand at room temperature about 30 minutes before serving. Makes 1¼ cups.

Nutrition information per serving: 536 cal., 18 g total fat (4 g sat. fat), 0 mg chol., 422 mg sodium, 89 g carbo., 5 g pro.

Berries 'n' Brownies

Berries 'n' Brownies

Just three major ingredients—raspberries, bakery brownies, and whipped cream—result in this fancy showstopper. If you have the time, go ahead and bake your own brownies.

4 cups raspberries
4 to 5 tablespoons sugar
2 teaspoons finely shredded orange peel
2 cups whipping cream
¼ cup raspberry liqueur (Chambord) (optional)
4 3-inch squares purchased brownies (such as milk chocolate, blond, or marbled brownies), cut into irregular chunks

Set aside 8 to 10 of the berries. In a medium bowl combine the remaining berries, the sugar, and orange peel. Spoon the berry mixture into a 1- to 1½-quart compote dish or serving bowl.

In a chilled medium mixing bowl combine whipping cream and, if desired, raspberry liqueur. Beat with chilled beaters of an electric mixer on medium speed until soft peaks form (tips curl). Spoon the whipped cream on top of raspberry mixture. Top with the brownie chunks and the reserved raspberries. Makes 12 servings.

Nutrition information per serving: 263 cal., 19 g total fat (10 g sat. fat), 69 mg chol., 63 mg sodium, 23 g carbo., 3 g pro.

Cookies and Cream

Choose your favorite soft cookie. Any type works as long as you can cut it with a fork.

½ cup whipping cream
2 tablespoons honey
½ cup dairy sour cream
24 purchased large soft cookies (such as ginger or oatmeal)
Honey

In a chilled small mixing bowl combine whipping cream and the 2 tablespoons honey. Beat with chilled beaters of an electric mixer on medium speed until soft peaks form (tips curl). Fold in sour cream. (If desired, cover and chill up to 1 hour.)

To serve, place a cookie on each dessert plate. Top with a spoonful of whipped cream mixture. Top with another cookie and another spoonful of whipped cream mixture. Top with a third cookie and the remaining whipped cream mixture. Drizzle with additional honey. Makes 8 servings.

Nutrition information per serving: 456 cal., 21 g total fat (10 g sat. fat), 43 mg chol., 310 mg sodium, 61 g carbo., 5 g pro.

Flan

You can find this well-loved inverted caramel custard imported directly from Spain on Mexican dessert menus everywhere. Traditionally used, canned milk gives flan a rich, caramel flavor.

⅓ cup sugar
3 beaten eggs
1 12-ounce can (1½ cups) evaporated milk
⅓ cup sugar
1 teaspoon vanilla
Fresh fruit (optional)
Edible flowers (optional)

To caramelize sugar, in a heavy skillet cook ⅓ cup sugar over medium-high heat until the sugar begins to melt, shaking skillet occasionally. Do not stir. Once the sugar starts to melt, reduce heat to low and cook about 5 minutes or until all of the sugar is melted and is golden brown, stirring as needed with a wooden spoon.

Remove skillet from heat and immediately pour caramelized sugar into an 8-inch flan pan or an 8×1½-inch round baking pan (or divide caramelized sugar among six 6-ounce custard cups). Working quickly, rotate pan or cups so sugar coats the bottom as evenly as possible. Cool. In a medium bowl combine the eggs, evaporated milk, ⅓ cup sugar, and vanilla.

Place flan pan or custard cups in a 13×9×2-inch baking pan on an oven rack. Pour egg mixture into flan pan or cups. Pour the hottest tap water available into the 13-inch pan around the flan pan or cups to a depth of about ½ inch.

Bake in a 325° oven for 30 to 35 minutes for flan pan (35 to 40 minutes for custard cups) or until a knife inserted near the center comes out clean. Immediately remove flan pan or cups from hot water. Cool on a wire rack. Cover and chill for 4 to 24 hours.

To unmold flan, loosen edge with a knife, slipping end of knife down side of pan to let in air. Carefully invert a serving platter over pan (or a dessert plate over a custard cup); turn dishes over together to release flan. Spoon any caramelized sugar that remains in pan on top. If desired, serve the flan with fresh fruit and garnish with edible flowers. Makes 6 servings.

Nutrition information per serving: 202 cal., 7 g total fat (3 g sat. fat), 123 mg chol., 92 mg sodium, 28 g carbo., 7 g pro.

Sweet Indian Pudding

A warm scoop of this cinnamon-molasses dessert brings a soothing end to your day. Be sure to spoon up every last bit of the sweet syrup you'll find at the bottom of the baking dish.

1 cup milk
⅓ cup yellow cornmeal
2 tablespoons margarine or butter, cut up
⅓ cup molasses
¼ cup granulated sugar
½ teaspoon ground ginger
½ teaspoon ground cinnamon
¼ teaspoon salt
2 beaten eggs
1½ cups milk
 Whipped cream (optional)
 Raw sugar crystals (optional)

In a medium saucepan combine the 1 cup milk, the cornmeal, and margarine or butter. Bring to boiling, stirring constantly; reduce heat. Cover and cook over low heat for 5 minutes. Remove from heat.

Stir in molasses, granulated sugar, ginger, cinnamon, and salt. Combine eggs and the 1½ cups milk; stir into cornmeal mixture. Pour into an ungreased 1-quart casserole.

Bake in a 350° oven for 1¼ hours. Cool on a wire rack for 1 to 1½ hours. Serve warm. If desired, top with whipped cream and sprinkle lightly with raw sugar crystals. Makes 6 servings.

Nutrition information per serving: 218 cal., 8 g total fat (4 g sat. fat), 89 mg chol., 217 mg sodium, 32 g carbo., 6 g pro.

FAST DESSERT IDEAS

Even if you're short on time, dessert doesn't have to be a lost prospect. Try one of these simple ideas:
• Fresh fruit sliced and tossed with a little honey and sprinkled with toasted almonds.
• A tea bar set up with several types of tea, lemon slices, milk, honey, and sugar, as well as purchased tea biscuits or assorted cookies.
• A cheese course that features a selection of cheeses and fresh fruits: ripe pears with blue cheese, berries and apples with Brie, and oranges with thin wedges of Parmesan.

Peaches 'n' Cream Ice Cream

The slight tang of cream cheese helps balance the sweetness of peaches in this smooth ice cream.

2½ cups half-and-half or light cream
¾ cup granulated sugar
½ cup packed brown sugar
2 beaten eggs
1 8-ounce package cream cheese or reduced-fat cream cheese (Neufchâtel), softened
2 cups fresh or frozen unsweetened peach slices, thawed
½ teaspoon finely shredded lemon peel
1 tablespoon lemon juice
1 teaspoon vanilla
2 rolled sugar ice-cream cones
¼ cup sliced almonds, toasted
Peach slices (optional)

In a large saucepan combine 1½ cups of the half-and-half or light cream, the granulated sugar, brown sugar, and eggs. Cook and stir over medium heat just until boiling; remove from heat. (Mixture will appear curdled.) Set aside.

In a large mixing bowl beat cream cheese with an electric mixer on medium speed until smooth. Gradually beat in the hot egg mixture. Cover and chill for 2 hours.

In a blender container or food processor bowl place half of the peach slices. Cover and blend or process until nearly smooth. Coarsely chop the remaining peach slices; set aside.

Stir pureed peaches, the remaining half-and-half or light cream, the lemon peel, lemon juice, and vanilla into chilled mixture. Freeze in a 4- or 5-quart ice cream freezer according to manufacturer's directions.

Remove dasher from freezer. Stir in chopped peaches. Ripen ice cream for 4 hours.

Meanwhile, for topping, in a plastic bag crush ice cream cones with a rolling pin, reserving bottom tips, if desired, for garnish. Combine crushed ice cream cones and almonds.

To serve, scoop ice cream into mugs or bowls and sprinkle with topping. If desired, garnish with ice-cream cone tips and additional peach slices. Makes 14 servings.

Nutrition information per serving: 241 cal., 12 g total fat (7 g sat. fat), 64 mg chol., 78 mg sodium, 29 g carbo., 4 g pro.

INDEX

METRIC INFORMATION

The charts on this page provide a guide for converting measurements from the U.S. customary system, which is used throughout this book, to the metric system.

PRODUCT DIFFERENCES

Most of the ingredients called for in the recipes in this book are available in most countries. However, some are known by different names. Here are some common American ingredients and their possible counterparts:

- Sugar (white) is granulated, fine granulated, or castor sugar.
- Powdered sugar is icing sugar.
- All-purpose flour is enriched, bleached, or unbleached white household flour. When self-rising flour is used in place of all-purpose flour in a recipe that calls for leavening, omit the leavening agent (baking soda or baking powder) and salt.
- Light-colored corn syrup is golden syrup.
- Cornstarch is cornflour.
- Baking soda is bicarbonate of soda.
- Vanilla or vanilla extract is vanilla essence.
- Green, red, or yellow sweet peppers are capsicums or bell peppers.
- Golden raisins are sultanas.

VOLUME AND WEIGHT

The United States traditionally uses cup measures for liquid and solid ingredients. The chart, top right, shows the approximate imperial and metric equivalents. If you are accustomed to weighing solid ingredients, the following approximate equivalents will be helpful.

- 1 cup butter, castor sugar, or rice = 8 ounces = ½ pound = 250 grams
- 1 cup flour = 4 ounces = ¼ pound = 125 grams
- 1 cup icing sugar = 5 ounces = 150 grams

Canadian and U.S. volume for a cup measure is 8 fluid ounces (237 ml), but the standard metric equivalent is 250 ml.

1 British imperial cup is 10 fluid ounces.

In Australia, 1 tablespoon equals 20 ml, and there are 4 teaspoons in the Australian tablespoon.

Spoon measures are used for smaller amounts of ingredients. Although the size of the tablespoon varies slightly in different countries, for practical purposes and for recipes in this book, a straight substitution is all that's necessary. Measurements made using cups or spoons always should be level unless stated otherwise.

COMMON WEIGHT RANGE REPLACEMENTS

Imperial / U.S.	Metric
½ ounce	15 g
1 ounce	25 g or 30 g
4 ounces (¼ pound)	115 g or 125 g
8 ounces (½ pound)	225 g or 250 g
16 ounces (1 pound)	450 g or 500 g
1¼ pounds	625 g
1½ pounds	750 g
2 pounds or 2¼ pounds	1,000 g or 1 Kg

OVEN TEMPERATURE EQUIVALENTS

Fahrenheit Setting	Celsius Setting*	Gas Setting
300°F	150°C	Gas Mark 2 (very low)
325°F	160°C	Gas Mark 3 (low)
350°F	180°C	Gas Mark 4 (moderate)
375°F	190°C	Gas Mark 5 (moderate)
400°F	200°C	Gas Mark 6 (hot)
425°F	220°C	Gas Mark 7 (hot)
450°F	230°C	Gas Mark 8 (very hot)
475°F	240°C	Gas Mark 9 (very hot)
500°F	260°C	Gas Mark 10 (extremely hot)
Broil	Broil	Grill

*Electric and gas ovens may be calibrated using celsius. However, for an electric oven, increase celsius setting 10 to 20 degrees when cooking above 160°C. For convection or forced air ovens (gas or electric) lower the temperature setting 25°F/10°C when cooking at all heat levels.

BAKING PAN SIZES

Imperial / U.S.	Metric
9×1½-inch round cake pan	22- or 23×4-cm (1.5 L)
9×1½-inch pie plate	22- or 23×4-cm (1 L)
8×8×2-inch square cake pan	20×5-cm (2 L)
9×9×2-inch square cake pan	22- or 23×4.5-cm (2.5 L)
11×7×1½-inch baking pan	28×17×4-cm (2 L)
2-quart rectangular baking pan	30×19×4.5-cm (3 L)
13×9×2-inch baking pan	34×22×4.5-cm (3.5 L)
15×10×1-inch jelly roll pan	40×25×2-cm
9×5×3-inch loaf pan	23×13×8-cm (2 L)
2-quart casserole	2 L

U.S. / STANDARD METRIC EQUIVALENTS

⅛ teaspoon = 0.5 ml	⅓ cup = 3 fluid ounces = 75 ml
¼ teaspoon = 1 ml	½ cup = 4 fluid ounces = 125 ml
½ teaspoon = 2 ml	⅔ cup = 5 fluid ounces = 150 ml
1 teaspoon = 5 ml	¾ cup = 6 fluid ounces = 175 ml
1 tablespoon = 15 ml	1 cup = 8 fluid ounces = 250 ml
2 tablespoons = 25 ml	2 cups = 1 pint = 500 ml
¼ cup = 2 fluid ounces = 50 ml	1 quart = 1 litre